FROM DUST TO TRUST

The story behind the Loiyangalani Trust

ANTHONY MITCHELL

O&U
Onwards & Upwards

Onwards and Upwards Publishers
4 The Old Smithy
London Road
Rockbeare
EX5 2EA
United Kingdom
www.onwardsandupwards.org

First edition, published in the United Kingdom by Onwards and Upwards Publishers Ltd. (2024).

ISBN: 978-1-78815-963-0
Typeface: Sabon LT

About the Author

Anthony Mitchell was born in London but spent most of his youth in Sussex, before moving overseas where he trained to become a Maths teacher. After nearly ten years of teaching, he returned to the UK, where he studied for and was awarded a Ph.D.

His final working life was spent doing the accounts for clients of a local land agent. He has now retired but still does some part time work.

A churchgoer from a young age, Anthony attended a variety of churches whilst overseas, but only really came to realise that there was more to Christianity than attending church when he returned to England. He attended religious festivals on a regular basis, always leaving with a number of Christian books to read. He now has an extensive library of Christian literature.

Anthony has also started a charity that raises funds for a school and the local community in a remote part of Northern Kenya. Much of his time is spent raising funds for the charity.

Other interests include long-distance walking and Bridge.

You can contact the Loiyangalani Trust by email at:
info@loiyangalanitrust.org.uk

Website:
loiyangalanitrust.org.uk

From Dust to Trust

Contents

From Dust to Trust

Foreword by Sophie Neville

The Scots branch of my family emigrated to East Africa from the Malay States in 1919 and, much like Anthony, I grew up to tales of great snakes and lightning strikes, despising the sight of tourists looking at lions from zebra-striped minibuses. I knew of the Omo river, read *The Dawn Stand-to* and learned what it was like to ride a camel. They can collapse beneath you like a deckchair. I did not know that Queen Victoria gave Kilimanjaro to the Kaiser as a birthday present or that there are quite so many wind turbines in northern Kenya.

My grandmother only just survived a devastating car accident in Nairobi. Her injuries confined her to Bedford, but she encouraged me to travel, saying, "Smell Africa for me." As a result, I found myself driving from London to Johannesburg in the company of three proficient mechanics and later made it back up to Lake Turkana in a clapped-out jeep. The dust somehow mixed with the excitement. I rode through Ethiopia, finding that precipitation can fall so hard that raindrops bounce three or four inches from the ground, and gained loathing of 'posho'.

At the turn of the last century, I crossed the Masai Mara on a horse. Our tents were raided whilst we slept, which annoyed me as my palm-top computer was swiped. Three years later, it was returned by a Kenyan student sponsored to study in Alaska. He'd read my documents, learning that I was engaged in aiding the people of Africa and, being deeply appreciative, had somehow got it back to me despite his wife's objections.

If we exist on this planet to help others, it is important not to make a hash of things and "cause utter devastation". Being a founder member of various health and welfare endeavours in South Africa, I've learned that setting up a small charity is not as easy as one might assume, but with trustworthy project leaders on the ground, a huge amount can be achieved with very little money. Sustainability is key. Running a school is a huge commitment. As Anthony has observed, "those seeking to change circumstances 'for the better' need to tread warily and consider carefully the results of any planned intervention".

'From dust to trust' is a fine mantra. Some might hesitate for good reason. The track is invariably hot and windy, the going sometimes rocky and prickle bushes scratchy, but when you are sustained by a spirit of gratitude and "find a path to the summit" the rewards can be amazing.

Those who give receive more than might ever be imagined. Uplifting others and helping young people to fulfil their potential is unexpectedly exhilarating. It is enlightening to read about what is happening in Lake Turkana and Loiyangalani, where goats and daughters are perceived as currency, clocks and calendars are unheard of, and a man's status is determined by how much livestock he owns. Those who inhabitant this volcanic, rocky area are stoic. Their children never get lost. You may be charged by women armed with water containers, but their singing will be melodic and the welcome they extend sincere. Buzzing menaces of the night might be a challenge, but the seeds of compassion sown can change lives and possibly a nation.

Let Anthony Mitchell inspire you to venture forth as he did. Be prepared to encounter circumcision rocks and swarms of small boys. Your tent may collapse and there will be crocodiles lurking in the shallows, but one thing is certain: life as you know it will be enriched, expanded and might become an inspiration to others.

Photographs

Family in Loiyangalani. The young man in the white shirt has been sponsored by the Loiyangalani Trust

Father Joya

Family in Loiyangalani, young lady in black trousers has been sponsored by the Loiyangalani Trust

Jacob

Loiyangalani Primary School

Bosco

9

Magdalene (left) and her mother, Laura (right)

Hut in Loiyangalani

The road to Loiyangalani alongside Lake Turkana

David

Children from Loiyangalani Primary School being
served lunch

Mother and child in
Loiyangalani

Fisherman with a Nile perch which he has caught in
Lake Turkana

Two young boys with their
wheelbarrow in
Loiyangalani

CHAPTER ONE

A 'Different' Safari

"I have decided that you should do the same safari that Mary-Anne has just completed," my cousin Peter informed me. Mary-Anne is his daughter.

This was August 1991, and little did either of us realise at the time the effect that this decision would have on either me or the people of Loiyangalani, a village in northern Kenya adjacent to Lake Turkana.

Peter, who has since passed away, was not strictly my cousin. He had been married to my mother's first cousin. My mother had been born and brought up in Kenya. My grandfather had been a prominent tea grower and made a tidy sum of money, having settled in the country in the late 1920s. The exact means by which he had earned his money, I never really discovered. I am sure he had had his finger in more than one pie! Ironically, I did not become at all familiar with the country until 1991. I had made a couple of fleeting visits prior to that which had involved participating in the regular safaris that are much loved by tourists from most countries. I had often observed lionesses basking in the shade looking at yet another minibus full of camera-snapping tourists, wondering why on earth they had become the subject of so much interest. There were to be no such opportunities on this particular trip!

I had never visited Kenya as a youngster, despite having grandparents and other family members residing there. I had never actually broached the subject with my parents as to why the Isle of Wight and then Malta were the designated destinations for our summer holidays.

In 1991 I was in the country to console my ninety-one-year-old grandmother, who had lost all three of her children in the previous two years, the last of which had been my mother, who had been knocked over and killed by a car while crossing a road in Nairobi. The car had decided to overtake a stationary queue of traffic and was consequently on the wrong side of the road when it struck my mother. Words like "diplomatic immunity" surrounded the incident as the driver was a member of staff at the American Embassy, so investigation into the accident was curtailed before it commenced.

Having participated in the more standard safaris, I was being offered an experience that was to be slightly more unconventional. At the time, I had not appreciated just *how* unconventional! The itinerary was such that it involved a seven-day excursion by 'truck', actually a four-wheel-drive vehicle of slightly dubious vintage, which was to take us north to Loiyangalani via Maralal, Baragoi and South Horr. We would then proceed further north to North Horr and return via Marsabit, Arthur's Post and Buffalo Springs. As it happened, the outward route was to become very familiar to me, but at the time, the towns and villages appeared and disappeared in rather a blur.

Most of my recollections in this book are taken from a diary that I have kept regularly over the years. There were, in fact, two trucks as we set off from Nairobi. We appeared to have stopped more times than scheduled because one truck was prone to mechanical problems. Little did I know at the time that vehicles with mechanical problems were to become a very significant part of my Loiyangalani story!

Over the years of travelling in Northern Kenya, I was to become very aware of the resourcefulness of the Kenyans. As will be seen, many of the vehicles that I had the misfortune to travel in were certainly well past their 'use-by date'! Luckily for their owners, but so not so luckily for their passengers, MOT tests are unheard of in Kenya. If they were to be introduced, this would certainly more than halve the number of vehicles on the roads! It was therefore obligatory to ensure that there was a mechanic on board for any journey of significant duration. These mechanics not only know their vehicles intimately but possess the resources to conjure up exactly what may be required for almost any mechanical fault, down to, in some cases, literally a piece of string! Breakdown services are not an option, even when in the vicinity of the cities. A decision to wait for the appearance of a knight in shining armour in the form of an organisation like the AA would be ill-advised to say the least. In fact, on the desert roads, waiting for any vehicle to appear could be deemed extremely foolish, given the scarcity of vehicles using some of these roads. Improvisation by the mechanic was the key to survival. Spare parts were in short supply, and luckily very little seemed to phase these wonderful young men. At least, if at all worried, they continued to smile at their passengers with an air of complete nonchalance!

On the first day of this expedition, it seemed to take us hours to vacate the suburbs of Nairobi due to numerous stops, some being prearranged, for example, the purchase of additional provisions, but others being due to matters certainly not obvious to the passengers. We eventually had lunch at a golf course, most memorable for being completely deserted in the middle of the day. Quite why this location had been selected, I had no idea. I was soon to learn that asking difficult questions more often than not produced nothing more than particularly vague responses. We continued through the afternoon. Eventually, we halted and erected the tents. Being in the middle of nowhere, we could only assume that we had in fact reached the intended destination for that day. I have never slept well on the first night in a tent, and this one was no exception. I was pleased to be roused at dawn for breakfast. Clambering back into the trucks, we proceeded to Maralal, where we were permitted to purchase items of our choice. For me it was fruit rather than souvenirs. I have always been particularly partial to passion fruit, which are plentiful and cheap in Kenya.

Lunch was taken at an oasis, where we shared the facilities with Samburu tribesmen, their goats and cattle – not too literally, I hope! We continued via Baragoi to South Horr. It seems as if the mechanical problems had been temporarily overcome, as we made good progress. In South Horr we were assigned a specific campsite which had the luxury of a 'bush shower'. Air conditioning in the vehicles could only be dreamt about. As it was very hot, windows tended to remain at least partially open, so much of the time we were covered in dust; a covering of dust being a small price to pay for a degree of air circulation. Consequently, a shower of any description was more than welcome. I noted that tent assembly was easier the second time round. Quite how difficult it had been on the previous evening I had neglected to record.

There appeared to be little urgency to leave on the following morning, and so we were entertained by the locals who very kindly treated us to one of their dance routines. Eventually, we were on our way again. Once the dusty road running north from South Horr has been negotiated, the road proceeds across a lava field. In fact, so little grows in the area that it is referred to as a "desert". Eventually one ascends an escarpment, at the top of which is the first view of Lake Turkana sparkling in sunlit splendour below. This is the "Ooh! Aah!" moment of the journey, so the trucks stopped and the obligatory photographs were taken (the facts about Lake Turkana have been summarised in the next chapter, where I set out a description of the lake and its history).

Before proceeding much further, we were asked to participate in the gathering of wood for cooking while we were in Loiyangalani. This would seem to be rather a bizarre task for tourists on safari in Kenya, but I was to realise the significance of this in later visits to the area. Although there are palm trees near the springs, it is forbidden for timber of any description to be harvested by the locals. As there are no other trees in the area, the local inhabitants are compelled to walk considerable distances to collect any wood they require either for cooking or house-building. The idea, on this occasion, was to ensure that we had all we needed for the cooking of every meal that was to be consumed while we were in Loiyangalani.

We arrived in Loiyangalani in time for lunch. We erected the tents and were shepherded to the 'Oasis Lodge', where we were permitted to use the swimming pool for a small fee! Supposedly a period of rest and relaxation followed – not that straightforward given the local climate. During the day, the wind never ceases in Loiyangalani, and it is, of course, very hot (a detailed description and useful facts concerning the village can be found in the next chapter).

After the siesta, it was time to explore the village. A group of tourists soon attracts the attention of the locals, especially the younger ones. We were soon accompanied by a group of children of various ages but also in various stages of dress or, more often than not, undress. The older children had a commendable knowledge of the English language and put it to good use. It was not long before we had been informed about the harsh conditions under which they lived and their desire to be educated in order to better themselves. I am certain it was a spiel that was used on all groups of tourists upon their arrival in the village. Nevertheless, it touched a nerve with me, and I mentioned to one of them that I would consider their plight with the possibility of financial assistance.

A peaceful evening was had by all, but a not so peaceful night by some. At 1 am I awoke to find that the roof of the tent was not where it was supposed to be. It was, in fact, draped all over me. My dormant companion was apparently oblivious to the whole situation, so I had to rouse him. Having extricated ourselves from the tent, my co-occupant and I managed to locate some string. I set to work tying together pieces that would ensure the tent remained upright for the remainder of the night. So much for the comforts of modern safaris! At least I had shown myself to be almost as resourceful with the tent as some of the Kenyans could be with their vehicles! Although sleep was attained, it was not a very restful night, with the thought that a second imminent collapse of the tent was most probable, and I was glad to emerge from the semi-chaos in the morning.

After breakfast, we were driven to the El Molo village which is about ten kilometres to the north of Loiyangalani. We managed to avoid the inevitable sales pitch from the women endeavouring to sell us their wares. We did notice that the El Molo people were shorter in stature than those from the neighbouring tribes and that they appeared to have serious tooth problems. Any dentist would have had a field day, but the poor patients would probably have been left with no teeth. The reason for the short stature and the tooth problems was the unsuitability of the water that they were drinking. As their nearest fresh water was in Loiyangalani, they were consuming the water from the lake. They had become accustomed to its salinity and were content to suffer the consequences. Because the tribe has become the focus of international attention over the years, I say more about them in the following chapter.

We were treated to a boat trip to one of the islands upon which there were crocodiles. Maneaters, they certainly were not! In fact, endeavouring to approach them for photographs was a signal to the crocodiles to initiate a mass exodus. Being apparently very camera-shy, they endeavoured to vanish as quickly as possible into the waters of the lake. We were permitted to walk round the island before returning by boat to the shore. I was to learn later that the lake does in fact contain some very dangerous crocodiles who are only too partial to a tasty morsel of human flesh as a delectable snack, but luckily for us, these did not reside on this particular island.

After lunch, we were left very much to our own devices. I walked to the side of the lake and watched some of the local fishermen who were hanging out the tilapia, a Kenyan fish plentiful in the lake, that they had caught. Once the fish had dried, they would be transported south and sold. It was not long before I had the company of one of the young lads that I had met yesterday. His name was Stephen. The possibility of funding for education had ensured that he would seek me out to pursue the matter further.

Little did he know at the time, but it was to be this encounter that would initiate my long association with the village. He decided that he would be my guide for the afternoon. He took me to a special rock where, according to my diary, they "carried out circumcisions and slaughtered goats", hopefully not at the same time! I think I was spared most of the gruesome details. Interestingly, endeavouring to find this particular location many years later was to prove fruitless. I am certain at the time Stephen genuinely believed he was showing me a site of local tribal significance. At that stage it never occurred to me that "circumcision" referred to a ritual performed on both male and female youngsters. The latter is more often referred to as female genital mutilation. Stephen did explain some of the customs of his tribe. I was extremely impressed by his command of the English language. He was probably about thirteen or fourteen years old, but still attended primary school.

At this stage, it is worth mentioning that, for a variety of reasons, the children in any one year at school, particularly primary school, are of different ages. Once we had returned to the campsite, I told Stephen that I would help him and his friend with the school fees that they needed to attend secondary school. The previous day he had been accompanied by a boy called David who had joined us when we returned to the camp. Although it was Stephen who persuaded me to become a sponsor, it would actually be David who would have the greater influence on subsequent events. Whether or not they believed that I would be true to my word, I have no idea. Stephen did write his name, David's name, the address of the primary school and the name of his headmaster in the back of my diary. At least he had given me the ammunition that I needed. I said my farewells to the boys as we were leaving very early on the following morning.

We had our supper and then retired for the night. The tent appeared to have been repaired during the day, the string had disappeared and an incident-free night ensued. Sleeping in Loiyangalani is never easy. The wind dies away at night, and although the temperature does decrease, it is not a very noticeable decrease when one is trying to sleep! No fan to circulate the air and certainly no air conditioning! Not sleeping at night was conducive to dozing at odd moments during the day. However, I find the more daytime dozing one does, the more difficult it is to have a satisfactory night's sleep.

I noted in my diary that I was grateful the tent did not collapse again during the night, as this enabled me to sleep more soundly than I had on either of the previous nights. We were up at 5 am, and breakfast must have been a rather fleeting affair because we set off very early in the day. The return journey was to be via Marsabit, but necessitated heading north to North Horr initially in order to reach the road that we needed. The early departure, as it turned out, was extremely fortuitous, possibly involving excellent foresight; one of the trucks had overheating problems which necessitated several unscheduled halts. We had to cross several dry riverbeds which contained potentially hazardous loose sand. Unfortunately, on one occasion the driver of the other vehicle failed to negotiate one such crossing and became firmly stuck in the sand. Luckily, there was sufficient manpower to ensure that it was only a minor delay. Extricating the vehicle by pushing ensured that sand reached any orifice on one's person that had not already been reached by the dust from the travels. There was a certain amount of brushing down, but it was only after the next shower that one could declare oneself "sand and dust free".

Lunch was taken in the middle of nowhere, probably an unplanned location. I did endeavour to doze during the journey, but the road was such that napping for more than a few seconds was impossible. I was to become very accustomed to being tossed around in the back of vehicles over the years. I am sure clothes have a similar experience in a tumble dryer. At least they are clean!

The campsite for this evening appeared to be more random than the previous one. I had been allocated a different tent, presumably because the previous one had been deemed to be in imminent danger of another collapse. However, I noted at the time that the replacement seemed to be no great improvement on the original one. Trying to find a suitable spot to erect the tent proved to be far from simple. I noted in my diary that the terrain appeared to be covered in "prickly things"; the precise nature of these significant obstacles was not recorded. As it happened, I had the best night's sleep of the whole trip, which may or may not have been viewed as lucky, considering our party was raided during the night. Fortunately, my tent was not targeted by the assailants. More than one of the other tents had had items removed and stolen. Stealth had been utilised to such a degree that no one had been disturbed during the raid. Thankfully, no one was harmed. I would imagine that a raiding party was less likely to be pursued by the authorities if it avoided harming the victims of the raid. Hence the fact that there were no casualties. It was as well that the incident had occurred on the return, rather than the outward, journey, as it would have instigated a distinct sense of unease each night as we bedded down in some remote location.

The following day was spent at Buffalo Springs, which is located in the Samburu National Park. This was probably the only day that came close to resembling the normal type of safari with an opportunity to view game and consume 'normal' food, including the imbibing of some most welcome cold beer. Unfortunately, the accommodation was not upgraded, and the tents were erected for the last time.

The final day was prolonged by further breakdowns, which seemed to cease once the tarmac was reached. We returned to Nairobi via Nanyuki. Despite having been roused again at 5 am, it was 5.30 pm when we eventually disembarked at the conclusion of what should have been a straightforward journey. The breakdowns appeared to have prolonged the journey significantly. Given the list of disturbing incidents to have experienced, we should perhaps have counted ourselves as fortunate that we had returned at all!

Upon entering my grandmother's flat, I headed straight for the shower. Apparently, I was in urgent need of both a shower and a shave. I had accumulated a considerable amount of dirt and dust, much of which took far longer to remove from my clothes than my body. Although the meeting with Stephen and David was the event that was to shape my future with Loiyangalani, it was the constant presence of the dirt and dust that, at the time, seemed to be one of the most immediate experiences of the trip. Looking back on the whole safari, I have wondered how the operators could have been permitted to conduct the expeditions with vehicles that were so unreliable. I am sure that it would not be permitted today. Any health and safety inspection would have rendered the expedition a non-starter. Nevertheless, my cousin had promised me an unforgettable experience, and it certainly was that – in more ways than one. The decision to support the two young lads would change my life.

It was to be over ten years before I was to return to Loiyangalani along those infamous roads, by which time I had all but forgotten about the potential discomforts and hazards.

CHAPTER TWO

Lake Turkana and Loiyangalani

Before continuing the story, this chapter will look in more detail at Lake Turkana and Loiyangalani, so that the reader has some indication as to the nature of the area in which the events unfolded. I will also include some additional information regarding the El Molo tribe and some comments relating to problems associated with schooling.

Lake Turkana

Lake Turkana is one of a series of lakes situated in the Rift Valley and is approximately three hundred and fifty metres above sea level. At present, the lake stretches for approximately two hundred and ninety kilometres with an optimal width of about thirty-two kilometres at its widest point. The deepest section of the lake has been measured at about a hundred and nine metres, although it is likely to have been closer to a hundred and twenty metres at the time of the last visit recorded in this book. For many years, the water level was receding at an alarming rate, but as I discovered on my most recent visit, the process has suddenly and inexplicably reversed during the last three years, so the volume of water is considerable.

It is worth elaborating on the contraction and recent expansion of the lake. Over the years, until about 2020, the shrinkage of the lake has most probably been occurring as a result of climate change. The situation has been exacerbated due to the fact that the main river in the north which feeds the lake, the River Omo, has been dammed by the Ethiopians, as the most northern section of the lake is situated within Ethiopia. Although they own a very small percentage of the lake, they do own the section in the north where the river runs into the lake. It is most unfortunate that the Kenyans have little control over the destiny of a beautiful asset. Complaints about the dam have apparently met with little sympathy from the Ethiopians. I believe that matters concerning conservation may not be high on their list of priorities!

Yes, the damming has assisted in providing the Ethiopians with land to farm in the south of their country, but the detrimental effect on the lake in Kenya has been ignored. The damming of the lake is a highly controversial issue and is an example of extremely selfish land management. It is very sad when countries cannot work together to ensure that any project has positive effects for both countries. If the rate of evaporation had continued, it would have been many years before the lake would have disappeared, but it has unique features, and an already vast area of desert would only have become much greater if the lake was ever permitted to vanish without trace. On occasions the rainy season can provide exceptional amounts of water, but with climate change this becomes less likely as the years progress.

As I mentioned, the situation has suddenly been reversed, with some devastating effects which I discuss later. I was to discover on the final visit recorded in this book that the water level in the lake had probably increased by as much as ten metres.

Explanations as to the dramatic change vary considerably. Although people have different ideas, there is no definitive answer as to the reason behind this dramatic increase in water level. The sudden reversal in the situation took everyone by surprise. I believe that climate change should be dismissed as a reason, since it was climate change that was supposedly contributing to the lake's shrinkage. Anyhow, the rise had been too sudden to contemplate this as an explanation. There had also been a drought in the area for the past two years. I discussed the situation with elders from the tribes, and they pointed out that there had been an earth tremor in Loiyangalani prior to the commencement of the rise of the water level. They suggested that perhaps the tremor had been more severe in the area to the north at the Omo River and that perhaps the dam had been breached. The dam may have suffered damage as a result of the earth tremor, but there is little evidence to support this theory. Alternatively, the Ethiopians may have deliberately permitted water to flow into Lake Turkana as part of a deal concerning the purchase of Ethiopian electricity by the Kenyan government.

When one considers that the lake is approximately three hundred kilometres in length, a rise of ten metres represents a vast quantity of water, so maybe none of these explanations account for the sudden rise.

It is worth noting that all the lakes in the Rift Valley had experienced an increase in water level. It may well be that the earth tremor had caused a fissure of sorts underground that had released a vast quantity of water. The general opinion is that the water level has now stabilised.

Lake Turkana is an alkaline lake with high levels of fluoride and therefore unsuitable for drinking, which, as mentioned previously, has had an adverse effect on the lives of the El Molo tribe. It seems that they have always drunk the water. It is not clear when they first became aware that it was the water that was the cause of their deformities. Members of the tribe suffered from curvature of the spine, bow-legged-ness and malformed limbs. Calcium deficiency has led to brittle bones, so much so that often their legs cannot support their body weight. Over the years, members of the tribe have received treatment for this condition, but this has only been achieved through sponsorship from generous donors, as the operation is highly specialised.

It was in 2008 that a project was initiated to ensure that El Molo had access to fresh water. Money was provided by grants from Europe and the Kenyan government. It was actually Jacob, who is the current headmaster of the Loiyangalani Primary School and at that time was the headmaster of the El Molo Primary School, who initiated the project. It is refreshing to note that most of the debilitating problems have now disappeared. Oh, that solving all problems could be that straightforward!

The lake itself has a plentiful supply of fish, mainly Tilapia and Nile Perch, the latter of which can grow up to fifty kilograms. There are also Solomon Fish, Tiger Fish and Mud Fish. I am not certain that there is much mud near Loiyangalani, so perhaps the Mud Fish are not so plentiful in this area. There are also crocodiles and turtles in the lake. The crocodiles seem to have shrunk both in size and number over the years. At least one of the early expeditions lost one of its members to a crocodile, but the crocodiles in the area around Loiyangalani appear to be considerably smaller and less aggressive. The man-eating crocodiles appear to frequent the northern section of the lake and at least one of the islands in the southern section of the lake. Apparently, the lake also contained hippopotami, but they have long since disappeared.

The first recorded visit to Lake Turkana by Europeans was the expedition of Count Teleki and Lieutenant von Hohnel which arrived at the lake in March 1888. The lake was initially named Lake Rudolf, after a crown prince of Austria who shot himself a year later as the result of a tragic love affair. Unfortunately for him, not only did he die prematurely but the lake that bore his name lost its original name and was later renamed Lake Turkana, a fate that was to befall the names of many other landmarks, not only in Kenya, but in many other countries in Africa. This first expedition proceeded along the eastern shore of the lake and passed close to, but not through, the present site of Loiyangalani. At that time, the area was teeming with wildlife and the lake was considerably larger than it is at present.

During the twentieth century, there were several expeditions to various parts of the lake. Should the reader wish to discover more about these, they are described in some detail in the well-documented and fascinating *Where Giants Trod* by Monty Brown. Perhaps the most tragic of the expeditions was that in 1934 led by Sir Vivian Fuchs. The expedition was to have been the first to circumnavigate the entire lake, but problems with the Ethiopian authorities, not for the first or the last time, refusing to grant permission to enter their territory resulted in a modification of plans. It was not until the 1970s that an expedition actually managed to circumnavigate the lake.[1] Due to the change in plans, time was spent studying one of the islands in Lake Turkana, the South Island. Two members of the expedition ventured on to the island to carry out various studies. They were well-equipped, and a system was established to allow them to communicate with those on the mainland should they require assistance. No signals were received, and the two men disappeared without a trace. Despite an extensive search of the area by boat and by air, nothing apart from a hat, two tins and two oars were ever found. These items were washed up on the western shore of the lake. The fact that the remains of their boat and two four-gallon buoyancy drums were never discovered added to the mystery regarding their disappearance. Their loss naturally brought the expedition to a premature termination. It was not difficult to understand why the crocodiles could have been the cause of their disappearance, as this is the island that is home to the man-eating Nile crocodiles. I was later to learn that some of the El Molo tribe had been residing on the island at the time. Blame for the disappearance of the two men had been erroneously attached to them. Although it was later realised that they were innocent, the British actually bombed the island in retaliation. This appears to have been an excessively dramatic overreaction, but it led to the inhabitants relinquishing their occupation and moving back to the mainland.

[1] See page 170.

Because of the problems crossing the Omo River at the north end of the lake, the early expeditions had focused on traversing the country on one side only, some along the eastern shore, others along the western one. As the whole area was inhabited by unfriendly tribesmen in the early days of exploration, the explorers used local guides, who were useful in finding ways to avoid encounters with local inhabitants who may prove to be hostile.

There is no doubt that the lake has retained its beauty but has changed considerably since it was first sighted by Count Teleki and his expedition. It is a very beautiful lake and often changes colour depending upon the nature of the light. It is due to one of these colours that it has also been called The Jade Sea.

The Village of Loiyangalani

The village of Loiyangalani is a relatively new development even in the comparatively short history of modern Kenya.

Loiyangalani, which means 'a place of many trees' in Samburu, is about seven hundred kilometres north of Nairobi, depending upon which combination of roads one chooses to use. It is approximately two hundred and fifty kilometres from the two nearest major towns, Marsabit in one direction and Maralal in the other. Most supplies are trucked from Marsabit, the larger of the two. Since my original journey, access to Loiyangalani has improved due to the building of a wind farm just south of Loiyangalani. This wind farm has three hundred and sixty-five wind turbines and makes excellent use of the constant 'hurricane' that seems to blow during the day. To reach the wind farm using the new road along the edge of the lake from Loiyangalani over the escarpment still requires negotiation, as during any heavy rains (notably absent in the past three years!) the road becomes impassable. In the past, sections of the road have been washed away, necessitating very interesting improvisations to reinstate its surface. The road has undergone significant improvement, as I was to experience on my most recent visit. It was not rain but the rise in the level of water in the lake that had necessitated the most recent improvised diversions at certain points.

Loiyangalani itself was first settled as a small British outpost between 1911 and 1915. It was then abandoned until the 1950s. The Oasis Lodge has been present in some form since then. It was originally known as Loiyangalani Safari Camp and was constructed in 1958. It was owned by Sir Malin and Lady Sorsbie. The camp was managed by Guy Pool until 1965, when the camp was attacked and overrun by a group of bandits called *shifta*. This was the raid in which Father Michael Stallone was killed.[2] A detachment of Kenyan police was sent to the safari camp to provide security for the area. They moved out in 1969 when a permanent police post was established in Loiyangalani.

In 1973 the name of the safari camp was changed to Oasis Lodge when the business passed into the ownership of a group of Italian businessmen. At the same time, there was a certain amount of rebuilding and modernisation. In 1980 the Lodge was bought by a group of Germans and is currently owned by a Kenyan. With this establishment attracting more and more tourists, it became a source of income for the locals, as they could sell their artefacts, charge for photographs in traditional costume and perform traditional dances for the visitors. Shops were then established mainly by enterprising Somalis. Unfortunately, the site has been neglected in recent years and does not offer the level of comfort for enterprising tourists that it was able to boast in its heyday.

The Consolata Fathers initially expressed an interest in establishing a mission in the area in about 1953, but it was not until the tragic death of Father Stallone that the mission laid the foundations for the first school and dispensary (medical centre). In 1966, the mission was fully established, with the Consolata Sisters arriving the following year. The missionaries established the primary school in 1967, initialling catering for grades one to three, and with the small dispensary offering basic healthcare.

It is worth pausing to consider the conditions under which children were learning prior to the construction of any classrooms.

Before the construction of buildings, children were taught sitting under trees in the shade. As the sun has the unfortunate habit of 'moving', so too did the shadow. Consequently, the children also had to move to ensure that they remained in the shade. Perhaps this was the original concept of 'mobile classrooms'! Obviously, when it rained or the wind was blowing excessively, school had to be adjourned. As it is windy most of the time, one wonders how often the children could actually sit outside and learn anything. Sitting on the ground could not have been comfortable. It is hard and unforgiving, with prickle bushes never far away. The children were also distracted by those who may have been

---

[2] See Chapter 11 ('The Consolata Missionaries') on page 161.

passing by. There was always the temptation to acknowledge the presence of an acquaintance. Who knows, even the odd goat may have had a desire to investigate what was happening!

Once classrooms had been constructed, the challenges did not evaporate. Desks were few. Often, five or six children would occupy desks designed for two. Those unlucky enough not to have a desk had to make use of the floor. Many of the children did not have access to basic necessities, such as books or pencils, so effective participation was often limited.

It was not until 1970 that the school was enlarged to cater for the additional grades. Meanwhile, students in the higher grades had to be transported to South Horr to continue their education.

In 1971 there was a solar eclipse. Scientists from around the world identified Loiyangalani as one of the best locations from which to view the eclipse, so there was a sudden influx of visitors.

Settlement from the local tribes accelerated during the 1960s. The original settlers were from the El Molo and Rendille tribes. The Samburu followed, apparently having discovered that the combination of the water from the lake and the salty soil in the area proved successful in deworming their livestock, surely much cheaper than any dewormer used anywhere else in the world. The Turkana followed in 1981 due to the Ngoroko menace in the area south of Lake Turkana.[3] The popularity of the area was due in no small part to the abundance of local springs. As mentioned previously, Lake Turkana, although looking very attractive, possesses water that is very brackish and unsuitable for drinking. The main spring in Loiyangalani has its origins in Mount Kulal which, standing at about 2,300 metres in height, is about twenty kilometres to the east of Loiyangalani. I was to become better acquainted with the mountain on my subsequent visits. The water has been piped from the spring to provide easy access for the villagers. The pressure in the pipe is so great that the tap must not be turned off. Halting the natural flow of the water would cause the pipe to burst. Of course, the first reaction of any conscientious tourist would be to do just that, so it is necessary to be aware of the situation before attempting to do one's good deed for the day and thereby cause utter devastation! This did not prevent me from a sense of unease at the sight of water apparently being 'wasted' each time that I walked past it.

[3] Ibid.

Trying to ascertain the size of the population of Loiyangalani is problematic. The people who come from three of the resident tribes, Samburu, Turkana and Rendille, are nomads. The fourth tribe in the area is the El Molo, but more of them later. Being nomadic, the people wander generally to the east of Loiyangalani with their herds, consisting principally of goats, searching for what little food they can find in an area in which virtually nothing grows. Consequently, the number of adults residing in Loiyangalani at any one time can vary from five thousand to over six thousand, in addition to the large number of children.

The basic food is *posho*, which can best be described as a form of porridge made from maize. Some of the more enterprising residents supplement their diet by catching fish. Traditionally, the nomads are meat and not fish eaters, so persuading them to partake of the bountiful supply of fish in the lake is not straightforward. The fact that the El Molo people are traditionally fishermen as opposed to hunters has caused them to be looked upon as inferior by their nomadic meat-eating neighbours. On occasions goats are slaughtered for family feasts. The fact that goats are the dominant 'currency' in the area ensures that the slaughtering of a goat becomes a significant event.

It is interesting to note that for a long time the locals struggled with the concept of 'money'. They understood that if their goats reproduced, then the size of their herds increased, and so this represented greater wealth. They could not understand that when they were given bits of metal (coins) and pieces of paper (notes) by the colonial settlers, these could be handed over to an individual in the local post office. Those depositing these items could return later to find that they would receive additional bits of metal and pieces of paper! Inanimate objects reproducing was beyond their experience. The whole idea of interest being earned on monetary deposits took a considerable while to be understood by the locals. Initially, it was regarded either as magic or stupidity on behalf of their new overlords. This was just one example of the difficulties incurred in trying to instil new ideas into a culture that had never experienced anything similar.

Houses are generally constructed using reeds.[4] The wealthier families do have more substantial dwellings.

During subsequent chapters I elaborate on the living conditions of the families and discuss the problems with which they are compelled to

[4] See page 55.

26

contend. Very little grows naturally, due to the hard volcanic nature of the rock. Apart from the rainy seasons, the climate is hot and windy, so living conditions can be very harsh.

The inhabitants of the village are very stoical and seem to accept their lot. The access to basic modern technology has revealed a world beyond the hardship of Loiyangalani. It is the hope of most of the families that one day their children will themselves be able to access and take advantage of this technology to improve their livelihoods.

The El Molo Tribe

The El Molo tribe is very special, found only in a small area north of Loiyangalani. It had established its own settlement long before the other tribes had ventured into the area. The tribe has been the subject of much research and concern. There is a strong desire to preserve the ethnicity of the tribe, but numbers are not vast and the temptation to intermarry with neighbouring tribes is evident. Although the tribe now numbers about a thousand, at one stage, it numbered less than one hundred. As mentioned earlier, they are a significant distance from the water supply in Loiyangalani and have survived by drinking the water from the lake. When I first visited these people, it was easy to think mistakenly that a child of fifteen was as young as nine or ten. The interesting feature of the El Molo community is their diet. Unlike neighbouring tribes, they have no animals. I have pointed out that they rely entirely on the fish from the lake, much to the disdain of the other tribes. Over the years this has been a distinct advantage. No stock, no raids! By and large, the neighbouring tribes have left them in peace as they have had nothing of value to steal.

The El Molo tribe has been the focus of attention over the years, which has caused it to flourish and ensured that it received funds to build its own primary school. However, at times, it has also struggled to survive. Unfortunately, as I discovered on my most recent visit, the significant rise in the level of the lake had marooned one of the villages so that it is now situated on an island; not very useful for a community that cannot swim and has few boats! Although the community remains where it is at present, it is thought that soon they will relocate to the mainland. The school is thankfully located on the mainland, but there is concern that if the level of the lake should rise again, the buildings will be under threat. The water is a matter of metres from one of the buildings, something that could never have been envisaged when the buildings were originally erected. The tribe has overcome many problems over the years, so I am certain that they can adapt to this latest predicament.

Establishment of the El Molo Primary School

The primary school was initially funded entirely by a very generous Austrian couple who visited the area many times over a number of years. Mrs Brigitte Meissel and her husband, Professor Wilhelm Meissel, first visited Loiyangalani and El Molo in 1984. They could see the need for a primary school in El Molo and set about raising money from their friends and colleagues in Austria. At that time, the nearest primary school was in Loiyangalani. This school had no boarding facilities, and expecting children to walk to and from El Molo was a non-starter.

Not only were the funds provided to construct the primary school, but there was also a boarding house, so that youngsters from nomadic families could attend. Because they realised that constant supervision was required, the Meissels returned to the area year after year to oversee the development of the scheme. By monitoring the progress of the project, they could show friends and donors in Austria the outcome of their generosity. Once the school was built, they ensured that it was staffed satisfactorily. In fact, the original headmaster, Jacob, first became the official headteacher at El Molo Bay Primary School in 1997 and, as previously mentioned, has since become headmaster of the Loiyangalani Primary School. He seems to bring success to all projects with which he becomes associated. Although the couple have both unfortunately passed away, their legacy lives on because they ensured that the project was sustainable.

Jacob has taught for a considerable length of time at both El Molo Bay and Loiyangalani primary schools. He shares my desire to ensure that as many children as possible have access to education in an effort to provide an exit from a cycle of life that perpetuates the poverty that is rife in the area. The situation can be likened to a mountain with very steep slopes to be climbed, but we hope to find a path to the summit!

As mentioned earlier, the majority of the children in the area belong to nomadic families. These families wander for miles searching for suitable pasture for their livestock. Their children cannot possibly attend school unless there are boarding facilities; no school buses to collect and then deposit a child to and from any particular point in the desert!

Jacob was extremely resourceful, with improvisation being the key to his success. There were three classrooms initially at El Molo Primary School. He decided that two of the three should be classrooms by day and dormitories by night. The girls were accommodated in the classroom at one end and the boys in the one at the other end. The middle one was vacant, except for a security guard who ensured no hanky-panky between the inhabitants of the other two! Sleeping materials initially consisted of mats, skins or even cardboard cartons; in fact, anything that was more comfortable than the floor of the classroom!

There were no showering facilities, just one tap. The girls were roused to use the tap first at 5 am and the boys followed an hour later. Further washing was permitted by allowing them to use the lake. Again, this was carefully supervised. The girls had one particular section, overseen by a designated teacher; the boys had another, again overseen by a teacher. Jacob was leaving nothing to chance, obviously fully aware of the hazards of mixed boarding facilities.

Eventually funds were received from the government and organisations such as UNICEF which provided equipment – beds, mattresses etc. – for the dormitories once they had been constructed. Separate showering facilities were also supplied, initially in temporary but later in permanent structures. The fact that the project was well-supported also ensured that there was a regular supply of food.

The school was so successful, not only in achieving excellent results but also by being in demand, that further classrooms were added so that students could remain there until the commencement of secondary education.

Challenges of Education

Being the only school with boarding facilities ensured that El Molo Primary School attracted children from the nomadic families, which gave rise to unique problems.

These families can wander up to ten kilometres per day and might be up to two hundred and fifty kilometres from the school at any one time. With families moving so quickly, how do the children find their families when they finish school at the end of a term? It was, and often still is, not a question of giving them a call to find out where they are. Phones do now exist but are not in the hands of children. Nomadic youngsters do not have the luxury of mobile phones! The children are extremely resourceful, making use of a form of 'bush telegraph'. By communicating with others along the way, they can ascertain roughly where they need to head in order to meet their families. It may take several days to find their family, but they never starve or die of thirst. According to Jacob, no child has ever been lost, which is incredible considering the distances and the conditions under which they have to travel. We have groups of children in the UK fully armed with maps, compasses and mobile phones who seem to manage to lose themselves in a square mile of the countryside!

A related problem concerns the return to school. The children have to leave their families and then trek across the wilderness, endeavouring to return to school as close to the commencement date of term as possible. Keeping track of the passing of the days constituting 'school holidays' cannot be easy without access to clocks and calendars. The whole concept of time is non-existent to nomadic families. There is daylight and there is darkness, but very little to distinguish one day from the next, unless it happens to rain which has not happened for some time. Why bother about a concept that has no bearing on one's way of life? Consequently, the return to school can be haphazard, to say the least. More often than not, it was the thought of a decent meal that had the children returning to school. Perhaps for some, it was the lure of a comfortable mattress on which to sleep instead of the hard rocks of the desert. There was generally a trickle of children arriving days, sometimes weeks, after the commencement date. Jacob would always welcome the stragglers with open arms. If any child was prevented from attending school for any reason, he or she might never return. Being turned away from school would be perceived as a form of rejection, and the parents would find something else for the child to do. Obviously, the more learning they missed, the greater the chances of having to repeat a year.

Flexibility was the key to encouraging children to attend school. A similar situation existed regarding the school year. The year starts in January, but for various reasons, children starting school may attend their first formal lesson at any time during the year. They are always welcomed and given the opportunity to familiarise themselves with the classroom routine and school system in general.

Ensuring that every child in each family should be permitted to attend school was not easy. Elderly members of the family have to be cared for. It is very common to have at least one child assigned by the parents to take care of and help with grandparents. Someone has to be the 'carer', a task that cannot necessarily be assigned to older members of the family.

This can lead to regular periodic absences or even the permanent withdrawal of a child from school. One cannot simply despatch an elderly relative to a local care home! It is not solely caring for elderly relatives that can keep children from school; there are household chores to carry out. For the nomadic families, the return of a child from school may coincide with an increase in the size of a flock or the loss of a member of the family who has been caring for the flock. The family may then require the child to remain with them rather than return to school. Care of the livestock is the number one priority for any nomadic family.

Perhaps of more concern is the whole issue of marriage. Daughters are still perceived in many families as 'currency'. They can be married off in exchange for livestock. They are seen to be a family asset. There is also an additional problem. Families are unwilling to pay for a daughter's education, because once the education has been completed, she will be married to a man from another family. Any costs associated with her education will have depleted her own family's livestock, while the benefits of her education will be used to enrich the family of her husband! This is of particular concern regarding secondary education, where fees have had to be paid. Jacob has said it has been common for families to balk at paying for the education of their daughters. It is more beneficial to receive a dowry for daughters when they marry, thereby increasing the number of animals owned by the family. The greater the number of livestock, the greater one's status in the community.

Jacob tells a story:

One very interesting case concerns a girl in Form Six, aged fourteen years. Her parents visited me in my office at El Molo Primary School. Her parents had given her away for marriage without my consent, after they had received gifts from her suitor. They requested to take the girl from school and bring her younger brother, who was not at school, as a replacement for her. Without this exchange arrangement, the boy would have no chance of joining the school. I asked them to keep their son at home and let their daughter continue with her education. Since they wanted to marry off their daughter and the plans would be messed up if she stayed at school, they insisted on taking her out of the school. I insisted that this was not possible, and they left very annoyed. Temporarily they shelved their plans, but later they executed them during the next holiday by taking her many miles away from El Molo and Loiyangalani so that I could not find them. I learnt about it once the girl had failed to turn up for the new school term. I tried to inquire as to where she was living, but I could not find her.

It is interesting to note the problems faced trying to educate children in a community that has very different customs than ours and a mode of living that is completely foreign to our way of thinking.

CHAPTER THREE

Touring with Father Joya

As I had promised the two boys, I sponsored them for the next four years through secondary school. I believe the fees were approximately one hundred pounds per year per student, so not comparable with any fees one might have to consider if supporting students at any private school in the UK! I am not sure why the fees were so low. The boys were both boarding, so it could barely have covered their living expenses, let alone the costs of the education.

Transferring the money was the most difficult part of the whole operation. Writing a cheque and then despatching it by post may appear to be relatively straightforward. However, the post office nearest to Loiyangalani was in Baragoi, some hundred and fifty kilometres south, from where the mail had to be collected and then transported to Loiyangalani. Not quite the same as having the mail delivered to one's door! I therefore enlisted the support of the Consolata Missionaries. Not only did they have a sizeable network of missions throughout the area, but they also had access to bank accounts. I will provide more information about this organisation in due course. Initially, the priest in charge at Loiyangalani was Father Lino Gallina, whom I was to meet in years to come. He was an Italian who spent most of his life in Kenya. For nearly four years, he ensured that the money I sent was received and passed on to the secondary school where the two boys were studying. When he had completed his time in Loiyangalani, he was replaced by Father Hieronymous Joya, a Kenyan missionary whom I would later meet and who was to become a great friend and supporter of all that I was doing.

In 1997, the paths of the two young men diverged. Despite having the early drive and showing the greater initiative, Stephen did not have the ambition of David. Stephen became a tour guide, then joined the Kenyan police. He seems to have parted company with them and has since disappeared off the radar. Unfortunately, I have not heard from him since 2003.

David decided that he wished to go to university. He gained a place at the Catholic University in Nairobi and needed a sponsor! Funding a student through university was a slightly different financial commitment from that of funding secondary school education. Needless to say, I decided that I would continue to sponsor him. The situation was further complicated by the fact that I could no longer rely on the Consolata mission as a go-between for the funds in Nairobi. Money had to be sent directly to the university, and for this I had to liaise with David. In 1998, I sent him the initial instalment of money required for his first semester. He was obviously a very persuasive and resourceful young man. He was elected by his fellow students as their representative on the student council for the university. The first year seemed to go well. Unfortunately, he then had to defer his studies for a year, as he was unwell. I never discovered the nature of his illness, but he managed to return to the university to start his second year of studies. In 2001 I sent him the fees for the semester and then all communication ceased. As time passed, I became increasingly concerned. Unfortunately, he was the initiator of all communications, as I had no contact details for him. Towards the end of the year, I received a letter from Father Gallina, who had been aware that I was supporting David. He told me that David had been run over and killed in Nairobi. He was unaware of the precise nature of the circumstances. I have never discovered exactly what happened. Considering my mother had been killed in a similar manner in Nairobi over twenty years previously, there was a certain irony to the whole situation.

I resurrected my association with Father Joya, who continued to operate in Loiyangalani, asking him if there were younger siblings in David's family whom I could help. David had a younger brother, Angelo, and sister, Magdalene. I paid for Angelo's secondary education, but he did not have the drive of his older brother so he failed to proceed any further. On the other hand, Magdalene was very similar to David. She had decided at a comparatively young age that she wished to become a nurse. I funded her secondary education and her training at Wamba Hospital so that she could achieve her goal. She has now completed her qualification, has married and works with her husband in one of the dispensaries in Loiyangalani. I have spoken to her on subsequent visits and am delighted that she has put her qualification to such good use. In turn, she is very grateful for all that I have done.

Father Joya completed his stint in Loiyangalani and was allocated a senior role in the Consolata mission in Nairobi. As part of his training, he was despatched to England to attend a special course in Kent. In July 2003, I was privileged to meet him for the first time. He had become very well acquainted with David's family in Loiyangalani and told me that his mother, Laura Daballen, was very keen to meet me, in order to show her gratitude for what I had done and was doing for her family (at this stage Magdalene was at secondary school). Father Joya was keen to renew acquaintances in the area, so he suggested that I return to Kenya and accompany him to Loiyangalani. He would very happily act as my chaperone.

It was not until November 2003 that I next visited Loiyangalani. Father Joya kindly met me at the main Nairobi airport. Having met him in England, locating him at the airport was not a problem; no need for those all-too-familiar signs being waved around in the arrivals hall, usually with a unique spelling of one's name! He then drove me to the Consolata Fathers' headquarters in Langata, not far from the centre of Nairobi. I had failed to remember quite what a nightmare it was to be in a car in Nairobi. I imagine drivers had tests to pass but did wonder as to the proficiency of those tests! When not stationary in the horrendous queues of traffic, it was simply a matter of driving as fast as one could for as long as one could and then stopping when one could proceed no further! Rights of way appeared to be virtually non-existent. If one had the courtesy to stop to give way or permit someone to merge into the main flow of traffic, one could be halted for an indeterminate period of time while more than one motorist took advantage of your generosity (or stupidity!). Failure to move at any moment in time apart from a red light generally resulted in a barrage of hooting from cars to one's rear. Although there were accidents, especially with the unbelievable *mutatus* (more of them later), I was struck by the fact that most Kenyans seemed to thrive in this situation. A special skill was the ability to fill an ever-shrinking gap in the traffic at great speed and live to tell the tale!

Eventually, we arrived at our destination in one piece, for which I was very grateful. I was extremely well accommodated and fed. There was a complete day to be enjoyed in Nairobi before we embarked on our travels north. Father Joya kindly chauffeured me round and then into the city.

Being able to park in the Catholic Cathedral car park was obviously a very useful perk from being a Catholic priest. Unless one arrived before dawn, finding parking spaces in the city centre was nigh on impossible. I was guided around the city and taken to the many stalls where I could purchase various items, whether they were a pressing requirement or surplus to one's basic requirements purchased due to the imploring look exhibited by the young female vendor. It was too easy to respond to the big smiles and 'pleading poverty' sales pitch by buying something one would never purchase under any other circumstances at any other location. It was also not long before I became conscious that in many of the streets I was the only white person. I was later to discover that one had to be cautious in the city, as one was particularly vulnerable to assault and theft. However, wearing his priestly attire, Father Joya was instantly recognisable as a priest and appeared to command respect wherever he ventured. Apparently, being seen as his companion seemed to offer me protection and render me untouchable. Whether true or not, I was never the object of any attack. Nevertheless, I was quite glad to return to the safety of the mission. I had a quiet evening preparing myself for the following day's expedition.

As I was to learn over the coming years, Kenyans appear to have little sense of time and can seldom be hurried. I do wonder how they manage to adjust when time does matter, for example, boarding an international flight, but they generally do. I had been advised that "an early start" was necessary for our trip to Loiyangalani. As events transpired, I had plenty of time for breakfast and the completion of the novel that I was reading. Initially, I was sitting in the front of the vehicle with Father Joya. Unfortunately, one never travels far in Kenya without passengers. Before proceeding any great distance, we had collected a "deacon" (a trainee for the priesthood) and a Consolata Sister, both of whom were travelling to Loiyangalani, so I yielded my prime position to the latter and relegated myself to the back seat of the vehicle.

There have been many criticisms of the colonial occupation of countries such as Kenya, and I will discuss them further later in the book, but the British did construct some excellent roads. Once independence was gained, maintaining these roads was apparently a comparatively low priority on the list of financial commitments. We often complain about the size of potholes in this country, but many of them pale into insignificance when compared with some of the chasms in the roads in the environs of Nairobi. One could do serious damage to life and vehicle if one were to encounter some of these at speed. At least most are very visible and easily circumnavigated. Do they prevent drivers speeding? Certainly not! Vehicles have brakes which can be applied abruptly if the driver is late in observing the hazard, even though one's passengers may be catapulted from the relative comfort of their seats. Interestingly, as often happens in the United Kingdom, the minor roads appear to be in a better state of repair. At least, once we were travelling along the more minor roads, there were fewer 'emergency stops' and I could admire the view without wondering when I would next be ejected from my seat. Eventually the tarmac road gave way to dirt. Apart from the inevitable clouds of dust, the journey continued in much the same manner until we reached the Consolata mission in Maralal.

I was shown my room for the night, which I was to share with the deacon. I noticed there was an absence of mosquito nets, but I was assured that any mosquitos we encountered would not be carrying malaria or any other nasty disease, so we were quite safe. For some reason, we were not offered supper at the mission and so the three of us ventured out into the town. Father Joya guided us to a café. This was probably the first time that I had eaten out in Kenya, so I was slightly apprehensive upon entering the establishment. The exuberant greeting that was extended to us upon entering the café disguised the fact that a possible failure in any health and safety inspection was probably an understatement. Hygiene did not appear to be high on their list of priorities. The menu was written in Swahili, so Father Joya ordered goat stew for three. What a treat! In my diary I recorded, "Goodness me!"

I was to eat goat stew on several occasions over the coming years. It was never to become a dish that I was to relish. The amount of meat varied considerably, depending on the circumstances under which the dish had been served. Suffice it to say, goats in Kenya are considerably leaner than those in the United Kingdom. The stew is also quite likely to contain wonderful pieces of the anatomy of a goat that would certainly not be served in the UK. I learnt that it was inadvisable to enquire as to exactly what one was eating at any given time. The term UFO – Unidentified Floating Objects – seemed to be appropriate to the contents of what I was being asked to consume. Many Kenyans view goat as a delicacy, so much so that when tackling the offering, every bone on the plate is stripped of any possible morsel of meat. Fortunately, stew is always accompanied by some item made from flour, usually a chapati of sorts. I was to be indebted to this addition to the meal on more than one occasion. I survived my visit to the café, but I did learn to be wary of what I should order in similar establishments in the future. It was easy to opt for a vegetarian style of living.

Visitors to foreign countries are often offered food they would never contemplate eating at home and one has to be very careful not to offend. When dining with the locals, the offering of a goat is considered to be a sign of real honour and a mark of huge respect. In fact, the slaughtering of a goat amongst poorer families is a rarity, as it represents a considerable portion of their wealth. It was unfortunate that I would happily have swapped goat stew for any amount of chapatis!

Once back at the mission, it was not long before we retired to have showers and slumber. This was the first of several nights over the years when I had to sleep without a mosquito net in a room that was most certainly frequented by mosquitos. As the mosquitos were not carriers of any nasty disease, such as malaria, they were not regarded as a potential threat to the incumbent. There is, however, a difference between the words 'threat' and 'irritation'. Attempting to sleep with a mosquito or mosquitos buzzing in one's ear is not easy, and all mosquitos are quite capable of imbibing one's blood! There was not a breath of air in the room, and to say it was warm would be an understatement. I had to develop a strategy to outwit the mosquitos. I could lie on my back with my body, including my arms covered by a sheet, but my head was exposed. I had to breathe. Due to the heat, I needed to inhale air that was relatively fresh. The solution was to cover my head with a towel. Luckily, I have a large proboscis, not usually an asset. I was able to use it in such a way that the towel suspended above the tip of my nose allowing me to breathe. The amount of skin exposed to the mosquitos was minimal, so provided that I could lie still, the threat from these annoying little creatures was nullified. Nevertheless, endeavouring to sleep under those circumstances was far from straightforward. Suffice it to say, I could have counted thousands of sheep and still been unable to sleep soundly. I was quite glad to see the sunrise and to be able to surface for breakfast.

There remained a considerable distance to travel before reaching Loiyangalani. Despite this, there was no hurry to leave in the morning. It is very easy to become frustrated by the apparent waste of time caused by the tardiness of the Kenyans. The solution is to adopt their attitude to the situation. Unless there is a very real deadline, there is no need to hurry. It was difficult, but I had to learn that (most of the time!) they knew what they were doing so I should relax. We now exchanged vehicles. The road north was to contain some interesting challenges requiring a vehicle that could withstand whatever obstacles might appear. Provisions had to be purchased. More passengers had to be accommodated.

Eventually, we departed. Almost immediately, the road deteriorated markedly. It had been raining, and sections of the road had disappeared. We managed to negotiate most of the very difficult sections. Unfortunately, there was evidence that one vehicle had not been so fortunate and had come to grief in a serious manner. One of the major hazards proved to be vast areas of water across the road. To describe them as 'puddles' would have belittled their size. 'Ponds' would have been a more realistic description. On more than one occasion, it was necessary for one of our intrepid passengers to disembark and test the depth of the water before we advanced. I had visions of him doing a 'Dawn French' in *The Vicar of Dibley*, i.e disappearing into a bottomless puddle never to be seen again. Thankfully, the water was never deep enough to trouble the 'tester' or our vehicle. Having successfully negotiated the road, we arrived in Baragoi in time for lunch. Again, we were entertained by the Consolata Fathers at the mission in the village. These missions are funded and maintained by the Order of the Consolata Fathers based in Italy. I have noted in the diary that we were presented with camel for lunch. It seemed to have been preferable to goat, but it was yet another interesting source of meat to be experienced, something else to be ticked off from the list of 'things I must sample before I die'!

Having been refreshed, we continued to the mission in the next village, South Horr. South Horr is very interesting in that it is a genuine oasis in the middle of nowhere. The village is situated in a gully between two ridges of mountains. The river flowing through the gully seems to contain water for most of the year. The climate and the fertile soil are ideal for growing various tropical fruits. In fact, when stationed in Loiyangalani, Father Joya had been so impressed with the ease with which things grew in South Horr, that he arranged for a truckload of soil to be transported to the mission enclosure in Loiyangalani in the hope that he could persuade things to grow there. Unfortunately, the growing conditions could not be replicated and so the project failed. To add to the two passengers that we had collected in Maralal, we gained two more in South Horr. I am uncertain as to how we accommodated everyone, but we did.

The road follows the river for a while. It is very sandy and dusty. Upon emerging from the gap between the two sets of mountains, one enters the Chalbi Desert. Although not a sandy desert, the Chalbi is very hot, very windy and contains little in the way of vegetation apart from Acacia. These bushes or small trees seem to thrive on a minimal amount of water. The terrain is very rough and in places quite rocky. The only animal that one is likely to see is the Dik Dik, which is a very small antelope. Other animals are present but are very elusive and rarely seen. There is an abundance of bird life. The birds in Kenya are very colourful and easy on the eye. Not being an ornithological expert, I was unable to determine the names of the different species encountered along the way.

There should be two iconic moments on this section of the journey, but it was dark so neither could be fully appreciated. The first is the initial view of Lake Turkana when reaching the summit of the pass over the escarpment. I had experienced this view on my previous trip. There was no stopping this time. The descent to the lake was as hair-raising as last time. Passengers hold on to whatever they can, but not each other! The road was in no better condition than on the previous occasion. Being dark, hazards seemed to have increased in size. The road follows the lake to Loiyangalani, but there are still small chasms caused by streams cascading towards the lake in the rainy season. These have to be negotiated with care, especially at night.

The second iconic moment is the first sight of Loiyangalani. The road rises over a small hillock and suddenly one sees the huts of the Loiyangalani residents scattered in the area below. Again, it was too dark to appreciate this. In fact, we had failed to appreciate this view on my previous expedition, and so it was a while before I managed to do so.

We headed directly to the mission where we were to reside. Despite the lateness of the hour, supper was provided (no comments in the diary as to what might have been consumed!). I was allocated a very pleasant room. There was again no mosquito net, but, joy of joys, there were no mosquitos either! I was most grateful for this and slept like the proverbial log.

Upon emerging from my room the following morning, I set off for an early morning stroll. I commented in the diary that "despite it being quite hot, there was a nice breeze blowing". One might assume that for a location near a desert in northern Kenya, with the proximity to the lake, the conditions appear to be close to idyllic! At this stage, I had not realised that for most of the daylight hours, Loiyangalani is very hot and there is an incessant gale blowing. The fact that the area is not only the windiest location in Kenya but most probably in the whole of Africa has seen the erection of the wind turbines mentioned in the previous chapter.

Father Joya had decided that the days were to be spent exploring the area. Our first expedition was to be to the village of Gatab, which is on the slopes of Mount Kulal. Although officially one mountain, it is an extinct volcano with a unique ecosystem stretching over an area of about eleven square kilometres, densely covered with trees. It is an incredible feature in the middle of a desert. As mentioned previously, it supplies the water for Loiyangalani and was part of Father Joya's domain when he was the priest there. Despite being probably less than twenty kilometres from Loiyangalani as the crow flies, by vehicle the distance is closer to seventy kilometres.

We reversed the route into Loiyangalani that we had taken the previous day, passing parallel to the lake and then over the escarpment. Eventually, we turned off the road and headed towards the mountain. Little in the way of formal engineering is evident in the construction of the road that leads to the summit. Not only is it perilously steep (I would not like to drive any of the trucks that are compelled to negotiate the gradient of the road in order to deliver provisions to the village), but it also contains blind hairpin bends. Without a horn, one could easily feature in a very nasty accident due to a significant drop from the edge of the road on one side. Fortunately, traffic is scarce, but an encounter with any oncoming vehicle, let alone a truck, is not to be desired. It was very much a 'hope and pray' road. Having negotiated the initial steep climb, the road then ascends alongside an incredible gorge with lush green vegetation, a delightful surprise considering the nature of the vegetation elsewhere in the area. The village itself is located some distance from the summit of the mountain. The unique microclimate allows the growth of tropical fruit. Ironically, it was raining when we arrived. Father Joya greeted his friends, but it was agreed that we should depart before the roads became an even greater hazard due to the rain. Slippery descents, hairpin bends and sheer drops do not make for pleasant driving!

As mentioned above, the road to Kulal is not a highway frequented by large numbers of vehicles, so the presence of a vehicle on the road is something of a rarity. There are small communities that inhabit areas not far from the road. Despite the rain within the mountain, the surrounding area is very arid, with little or no water for the majority of the year. Vehicles such as ours always carried significant quantities of extra water.

I was soon to find out why. When vehicles are sighted by the inhabitants of these communities, there is a mad sprint to reach the vehicle before it passes. Bearing anything that might hold water, women and children of all ages flag down the vehicle, seeking as much water as can be spared by the occupants of the vehicle. On more than one occasion, the vehicle in which I have been travelling has stopped to provide this commodity. These people appear to be so desperate that I wonder how they survive when there are no vehicles.

On this occasion, we were set upon by women and children appearing from nowhere, fortunately armed with nothing more threatening than water containers of various descriptions. We dispensed a significant quantity of water, for which they were most grateful. We also chanced upon a young lad, probably aged between twelve and fourteen, hobbling along the track on his own. He had been bitten by a snake while minding the family's goats. He was walking about fifty kilometres to seek treatment. I can only assume that the bite was painful but not deadly; there are some deadly snakes in the desert. This situation highlighted the dangers faced by the young lads minding herds of goats on their own in the middle of nowhere. If one such youngster has an accident of any sort or is bitten by anything venomous, he either sits down and dies or else attempts to walk a considerable distance to seek medical attention. Phoning for an ambulance is not an option when one is in the middle of a desert! It is chilling to realise that even today, young lads still live under these conditions, minding goats on their own. As will be discussed later, this is one of the reasons why the charity that I have set up is endeavouring to put an end to this practice by offering these youngsters education in the hope that it will improve their lives.

On our return to Loiyangalani, we had lunch. I was then despatched to explore the village. This gave me the opportunity to find Magdalene's home. Despite not speaking a word of any of the local languages, it was not difficult to seek guidance as to where the home was located. Everyone appears to know everyone! Visiting her house and meeting her mother was, after all, one of the main objectives of the visit. On reaching my destination, I was pleased to find that both Magdalene and her mother, Laura, were in residence. Introductions were unnecessary from either party. Although we had never met, everyone in the village seemed to know me and the reason for my visit. The sheer ecstasy with which I was greeted by Laura left me in no doubt as to her identity. Magdalene was less ebullient, being very shy, but nonetheless pleased to meet me. Words poured forth from Laura, none of which I had a hope of understanding. Poor Magdalene had to slow down the outpouring and take on the role of interpreter. Communicating via an interpreter is never easy, especially when one party scarcely draws breath between sentences.

Laura was probably in her sixties or seventies; it was hard to tell. She was extremely wobbly on her knees and did, at one stage, ask for money for a hospital visit to remedy the situation, but I was informed that there was probably little that could be done. She gave me a bracelet which I have kept. It was not the most intricate of gifts, but she had obviously taken the trouble to make it herself, despite her physical problems. It is gifts like this that are worth more than gold. To me it was a generous token of her gratitude. Father Joya soon arrived and escorted me back to the mission, but not before we had accepted an invitation to return the following evening to dine with the family.

The following day, Father Joya decided we should travel north to El Moite, another outpost which had been part of his domain. I have failed to find this village marked on any map, but the road was no worse than any other in the area, proceeding for the most part along the edge of the lake. Word of our approach appears to have preceded us. We were met by a considerable number of the inhabitants of the village while still on the approach. It was becoming obvious that Father Joya had made a lasting impression on the local inhabitants in all the villages in the area. He was always greeted with great affection. Once in the village, mass was celebrated. The size of the turnout may have been a reflection of the strong Catholic faith there, but it could also have been due to Father Joya's magnetism. We then had lunch, which I have recorded as being "*posho*" which, as I mentioned earlier, is the staple diet of most families, with no hidden surprises. I do have a photo of Father Joya dancing with a small group of locals that included the local witch doctor. The mind boggles! It shows that cultural beliefs often exist hand in hand with the introduced religious beliefs. I will discuss this again later.

On the return journey, we stopped at the village of El Molo, a detailed tour which gave me an insight into the problems encountered by these people, as discussed earlier in this book.

The evening was spent as guests of the Daballen family. A goat had been slaughtered in my honour. Being very naïve, at that time I failed to appreciate the significance of the event. A family's wealth is determined usually by the number of animals, usually goats, that it possesses. Assets such as huts and meagre possessions do not contribute to a family's wealth. Many families possess less than fifty animals, so the killing of a goat represents a significant sacrifice by the family. It was indeed a great honour, but it was so difficult to enjoy consuming something that was close to being unpalatable. I am certain that those confronted with similar situations on a regular basis have developed suitable strategies to ensure that diplomacy prevails. I was confronted with a serving that contained copious amounts of gristle but very little meat. Not only that, but there were various other aspects of the goat's anatomy floating around (lots of UFOs!), some of which I was informed were fried intestines! Most of the sordid detail was not revealed until I had attempted to consume as much as I could without offending the family. The meal was accompanied by chapatis, which were excellent. It was genuinely upsetting to understand the sacrifice that had been made without me being able to fully enjoy it. Hopefully, I managed to cause no offence to the family. I have fond memories of Laura, who was clearly struggling with her health.

This scenario was caused by the huge socioeconomic gulf between the Daballen family and me. It had been a comparatively minor sacrifice for me to provide the funds to educate David, Angelo and Magdalene, and yet the family had made a far greater sacrifice to entertain me. My generosity had been insignificant compared with theirs, something I could comprehend but they could not. I was to learn again and again the kind-hearted and generous nature of the Kenyans, particularly those from poorer backgrounds in the rural areas. It is relatively simple for those from affluent nations to help those from poor countries in small but significant ways that can change their lives for the better. Experiences like this have certainly changed my attitude towards life, and I believe that more people should engage in similar situations.

The following day, being Sunday, I attended mass in the Catholic church in Loiyangalani. I was to attend several such services over the years, and I made several observations as a result. Do not turn up early! The benches upon which we sat were hard, with no cushions or padding of any sort. It is Kenya, so the service commences when the priest decides that the number of attendees is sufficient to permit the service to proceed. This can be anything up to thirty minutes after the scheduled commencement, by which time one's posterior is beginning to suffer! As it happens, the congregation continues to increase as the service progresses. Fortunately, there is a group of singers with excellent voices who produce a memorable introduction to the proceedings. The time from arrival to departure can easily exceed two hours. On the whole, children behave immaculately. There is no running around, no chatting and no noise. Even amongst the very young, there appears to be an understanding that they are expected to be silent. Although there is no standard dress code, the adults and older children wear their best attire. The singing throughout is unbelievable. Perhaps it is only those from outside Africa who may be tone deaf or unable to hold a tune, but all Kenyans appear to be able to sing melodically. There is no written music, but the harmonies would impress the keenest musician. Perhaps those who cannot sing tunefully do not sing, but to me the sound was impressive.

Giving to the collection appeared to be mandatory. Only Kenyan shillings are acceptable, so giving in kind is out of the question. This may seem obvious, but it had been not many years since taxes had been paid in goats, cattle and camels! Even the poorest families were expected to part with a few coins. I failed to establish whether the giving was spontaneous or whether it was expected as part of an attendance 'levy' for participating in the service.

The service was conducted in Swahili, so my understanding was fairly limited. Nevertheless, I was very moved. The atmosphere was such that the congregation appeared to be deeply involved in the proceedings. Father Joya had been invited to officiate at this service, so inevitably I was introduced to the congregation in Swahili with what I can only hope were very positive words! Fortunately, the reaction of the congregation seemed to suggest that this was the case! I then had to respond, which was not difficult. My English was probably comprehended by a significant proportion of the congregation, but there was an interpreter at hand to ensure that the message reached all attendees.

The plan was to commence our journey south immediately after the service. Inevitably, our start time was delayed as farewells were exchanged. The visit had had a profound effect on me. I had noted in my diary that it had provoked within me a strong desire to do more than assist in the education of one family.

We had a late lunch in South Horr and drove to the mission in Baragoi for the overnight stay. The facilities were not as good as those in Loiyangalani. I had to endure a cold shower, during which there was a power cut. I had to extricate myself from the shower, dry myself and navigate my way back from the shower block to my sleeping quarters in complete darkness. I did remark in my diary that I had the luxury of a mosquito net, so no erection of barricades to outwit unwanted buzzing menaces during the night!

After breakfast, we resumed our journey to Maralal. We collected one or two extra passengers along the way. Whether their involvement in our journey had been pre-planned, I have no idea. Hopefully, each individual was known to Father Joya or one of the other passengers. I had complete trust that we were not about to be hijacked by undesirables at any stage. Once in Maralal, we deposited all the passengers and changed vehicles. For the remainder of the journey, I had the luxury of a front seat, something I had not enjoyed previously. There were no additional passengers on this section.

The journey to Nairobi was uneventful. I lodged at the Consolata mission for the night. On the following day, I said my farewell to Father Joya, promising him that I would make a positive contribution regarding Loiyangalani. I was collected by my cousin, Peter, and driven to his house in Naivasha. Board and lodging there was of a significantly higher standard than it had been during the earlier part of my visit to Kenya. I became a pampered tourist for a few days before returning to England.

Undoubtedly, this visit to Loiyangalani had had a more profound effect than the first. Being able to spend time with the people in the area had given me an insight into the needs of the community. Visiting areas that are not only remote, but predominantly unaffected by tourism, gives one a deep understanding as to how the local inhabitants survive in their environment. It was not easy to determine how, as an individual, I could provide meaningful assistance in more than a minimal manner. The seeds of desire were sown and then had the opportunity to develop when I returned home.

CHAPTER FOUR

Inspired by Sister Elizabeth

My next visit to Loiyangalani was in March 2005. On the previous visit I had had a long discussion with one of the Consolata Sisters based in Loiyangalani, Sister Elizabeth. She had suggested that I return to Loiyangalani and spend time with her, as she had ideas for ways in which I could help the community.

Sister Elizabeth, like Father Joya, is Kenyan. She was very keen that the women in Loiyangalani become self-sufficient. She was looking for schemes whereby they could sell their produce. She informed me that she could arrange to meet me in Nairobi and organise transport to and from Loiyangalani. It all sounded so amazingly straightforward. As so often happens in Kenya, events rarely pan out in the way that one anticipates!

Father Joya met me at the airport, and I stayed at the Consolata Seminary, as distinct from the Consolata mission. I was again very well looked after. I decided that I would like to take items to Loiyangalani that could be distributed to the children. After some discussion, we decided upon apples. Not only are they nutritious, but they are durable and hence more likely to survive the rigours of road travel to Loiyangalani. Father Joya took me to a local store and the bargaining commenced. I am sure the proprietor had never before sold quite so many apples to one customer. I purchased three cartons and was very satisfied with my negotiating skills.

Although being accompanied by Sister Elizabeth, the journey north was not in a vehicle belonging to the Consolata community. We were to be driven by one of the aid agencies or Non-Government Organisations (NGO). I had been given very precise instructions to be in their offices in Nairobi by 8 am the following morning in order to facilitate a swift departure. I had an early breakfast, and Father Joya kindly braved the early morning traffic to ensure that I arrived in good time. We collected Sister Elizabeth en route. Upon reaching the office, it became very clear that there was an absence of any vehicle likely to transport us in a northerly direction. Quite where it was, I have no idea. Four hours passed before it eventually arrived. As usual, requesting an explanation for the delay was met with blank stares. Thank goodness for a good book to read to pass away the time! There were five passengers, and so I was again assigned to the rear of the vehicle, a place to which I was becoming very much accustomed. Negotiating the traffic out of Nairobi was very frustrating. To describe the driver as ultra-cautious would be an understatement. At least there was no danger of incurring a speeding fine! Progress was indeed quicker when the tarmac eventually gave way to dirt.

Lunch was non-existent, probably as a result of the late departure, so I was ready for food when we eventually reached Maralal. Thankfully, Sister Elizabeth had organised accommodation at the Consolata mission. It seemed common practice for the Fathers and Sisters to have distinct facilities in the mission compounds, so much so that they even ate in separate quarters. On this occasion, I was very much a guest of the Sisters and therefore used their facilities. After a very satisfying meal, I was content to retire to my room and read for a while. Again, there was the lack of a mosquito net, which was frustrating as I was therefore compelled to do battle with the mosquitos. My tactics were inevitably similar to those employed on the previous trip. At least I could erect the defences immediately without the need for experimentation. The result was yet another poor night's sleep. I was to learn that mosquito nets were generally only supplied if the mosquitos were thought to carry malaria.

After breakfast, Sister Elizabeth and I rejoined our fellow travellers. As previously, a more robust vehicle was required for the remainder of the journey. The number of passengers had not diminished, but the amount of space had. I was squeezed into the rear of the vehicle. Seating for three had to be adapted to accommodate four. I was extremely uncomfortable, and in my diary I described the remainder of the journey as being "an ordeal". We had again departed rather later than was expected, so lunch was taken at a café in Baragoi. My previous experience had prompted me to decline the rather dubious looking stew. Instead, I opted for the chapatis. We then continued to South Horr, where we were permitted a short break. By this time, we had become wedged into the vehicle in such a way that disentangling ourselves from the rear required a considerable effort. We then proceeded to Loiyangalani. There were no stops for any picturesque views. In fact, I was more than grateful to reach the mission in Loiyangalani where I managed to extricate myself from the rear of the vehicle for the final time. I think my apples had had a far more comfortable journey! At least I had not had to face any additional charges for their transportation.

With no Father Joya, I was in the hands of the Consolata Father in charge, Father Evarist. When in the hands of the Consolata Fathers, I have always been well looked after, but for some reason, on this occasion I was not permitted to reside in the guest room in his building. I was banished to the 'guest quarters'. I am uncertain as to how often these rooms are used. Using the shower and toilet involved an outdoor expedition from my bedroom, which was fine when there was sufficient illumination to see where I was going; any excursion during the night was less straightforward as the electricity generator did not operate during the night.

After supper I ventured over to the Sisters' quarters and discussed plans with Sister Elizabeth for the following day. I then returned to my room to experience the delights of residing in the 'guest quarters'. Switching on the light in the bedroom revealed that I was apparently sharing the room with scorpions. This was an unexpected surprise! These delightful creatures tend to emerge when it is dark. Upon switching on the light, the few that had taken up residence made a swift exit. I surmised that provided a visit to the little boys' room was not required during the night, I was probably safe from any confrontation should I remain in my bed. The scorpions were small, so attempting to climb up the legs of my bed would be doomed to failure. I then proceeded to the shower room to find that a scorpion had lodged itself in the plug hole of the basin. It took an immediate dislike to the running water when I turned on the tap. It somehow managed to scurry up the side of the basin and leap on to the floor, disappearing never to be seen again.

The shower was yet another interesting experience. There is no hot water in Loiyangalani. The water temperature is such that all showers are refreshing but not too cold and generally the pressure is constant. Unfortunately, on this occasion my ablution room was some way from the main storage tank for water at the mission. In my diary, I state that I had a "shower of sorts". The water pressure was such that showering was not the delight that it usually was when visiting Loiyangalani.

I returned to my room, which appeared to have been vacated by the scorpions. The room was airless and so sleeping was again a challenge.

At least I had monitored my intake of fluids in such a way that there was no need to venture out from my room during the night!

Shaving in the morning was yet another interesting experience. Plugs for basins appear to be an optional extra rather than a necessity. Therefore, filling the basin with water to shave required improvisation. Bereft of anything resembling a plug, I was compelled to use my flannel, which stemmed the flow of water exiting the basin sufficiently to allow me to remove most of the growth around my face. After my interesting experiences, I was relieved to join Father Evarist and his assistant for breakfast.

Sister Elizabeth and I were then driven to the village of El Molo, where we spent the morning. On this visit with Sister Elizabeth as my interpreter, I was able to discover a little more about these people. They are keen to preserve their identity and avoid intermarriage with the neighbouring tribes where possible. They are aware of the interest that has been generated overseas by their plight. They have been visited by various people and are very much on the 'must-see list' for any tourists visiting the area. Not only are they adept at presenting themselves but also very quick to demand fees for any photographs. As soon as we arrived, women emerged from huts with a vast array of basketry and beaded items. These were spread out on the ground for my perusal. There is no doubt that the craftsmanship was highly skilful. Sister Elizabeth explained that I was interested in buying items to take back to England to sell on their behalf. Obviously, the beaded items, mainly bracelets and necklaces, had caught my eye. Although the basketry was excellent, space in one's luggage was limited. There was, though, a significant problem. I had limited cash and I was hoping to purchase items 'on account', with a view to sending them the money once the items had been sold. The idea that I could most likely sell the items in England for more than their asking price in the village was an extremely difficult concept to explain.

Sister Elizabeth understood my idea, but she had great difficulty persuading them that nothing now would lead to more later. Unfortunately, they needed money now and would not allow me to take anything on a 'pay later' basis. Consequently, I purchased a few of their wares, but nowhere near the number of items that I had intended. I was to have better luck with a group of women in Loiyangalani.[5]

[5] See page 62.

I was given a thorough tour of the village. I observed a fisherman hauling in what I judged to be an enormous Nile Perch. I have no idea of its weight, but it was over a metre in length. When I congratulated him, he responded, through Elizabeth, that it was not the biggest he had caught. Apparently, they do grow considerably larger. In fact, it was the size of these fish that attracted the first tourists to the area. At that time fishing trips had been organised in boats that ventured further out on to the lake. The El Molo fishermen usually fish from the shore using hand lines and live bait. The perch are not difficult to land as they are not renowned for their fighting spirit. No visions of poor fishermen being dragged into the lake desperately trying to haul in their catch!

While in the area, I was shown a desalination plant. One well-meaning organisation had become very concerned about the effect that the drinking of the water from the lake was having on the El Molo people. It was decided that a desalination plant would be given to them so that the water could be rendered drinkable. The plant was assembled, and for a while the El Molo people had excellent drinking water. Unfortunately, the climate, the wind and the dust are not kind to machinery such as this. The plant soon gave up the ghost. Although the Kenyans are very good at improvisation, there was only so much they could do. They did not fully understand the workings of the plant and were uncertain as to which new parts were required to fix it. For various reasons, those involved in the original scheme could not be contacted. The plant remains a memorial to good intentions!

Unfortunately, this is a saga that is often repeated in developing countries. Later, I will refer to another project that was funded and commenced with the best of intentions but for various reasons never fulfilled its potential. Sustainability is a key word in the implementation of any scheme or project. Often, there is a strong desire to assist those in need. Before one decides to commit to any new project, there is the need to establish the long-term sustainability of the plan.[6]

As will be seen, I have sometimes perhaps acted a little overzealously, with the result that some of my ideas have turned out to be less sustainable than I originally had hoped. It is very easy to show enthusiasm for an idea which generates hope and excitement, but then founders because one element of the scheme is unsustainable.

---

[6] See Chapter 13 ('Support and Sustainability') on page 184 for further discussion.

The afternoon was spent in the company of Sister Elizabeth. She gave me a comprehensive tour of Loiyangalani. I was able to meet people and listen to their stories. I again had supper at the mission. I then disappeared to my quarters to negotiate the perils of the washroom and then my bedroom. The shower remained obstinate in its reluctance to part with more than a trickle of water. One or two scorpions apparently still believed they should be entitled to share my sleeping quarters until blinded by the light, my secret weapon, that persuaded them to scurry away to find more favourable hiding places.

The following day, Sister Elizabeth took me to the two nursery schools and the primary school. The nursery schools had been funded and constructed by the Consolata mission, and both were staffed by Consolata Sisters. Each consisted of a single room within a thatched hut. Technically, they were, therefore, privately run. To call them 'private' nurseries, however, could easily convey the wrong impression, as private schools in most countries are not only independent but also demand the payment of school fees. These nursery schools were non-fee-paying. The huts were locked each night, supposedly to safeguard them against unwanted intruders. This ploy was very successful against those of a human nature, but not so successful against those of other types. Each morning the Sister-in-charge had the dubious task of persuading unwelcome overnight visitors, such as snakes, that they should vacate the premises before the children entered. Fortunately, they usually obliged with the minimum of fuss. Each hut contained very little in the way of furniture. The children sat on the ground; no carpet or matting!

The first task each morning involved a recital of the English alphabet using an illustrated chart that depicted items whose names commenced with each of the letters of the alphabet. The first illustration was "A – Apple", so the children chanted, "A is for Apple." Imagine their surprise when I entered their nursery with apples! Given that before my arrival, these children had never set eyes on an apple, how could a well-meaning teacher possibly convey to the children the concept of an 'apple'? Yes, the picture showed them that it was green, spherical and looked inviting. One might categorise the apple as being a fruit, but remember that the children live on maize, possibly the odd piece of goat or fish. They had never seen any varieties of fruit, so developing a meaningful concept as to the nature of an apple was nigh on impossible. Until now! I had arrived with a large box. What was in my box? Apples! When purchasing the apples, I had no idea that I would be providing a concrete aid to a lesson on the alphabet! Unfortunately, providing concrete aids for "X – Xylophone" was beyond even my capabilities! The apples were distributed, but of course, the children had no idea what to do with them. Were they missiles to be hurled at each other? Were they an interesting type of ball with which to play 'catch'? The Sister-in-charge explained how they were to be tackled. Once shown, the children had no hesitation in taking their first bites. There was no evidence of any apprehension amongst the children as to what they were being asked to do. Unlike children from affluent countries, they had probably never eaten anything that they disliked, so they assumed that anything to be eaten must taste good. As it happened, there was never any doubt as to what they would think of the apples; the expressions on their little faces were those of pure joy. Perhaps this was most evident when I later walked amongst their huts, always to be pointed at and greeted by, "A is for Apple!" Maybe they thought that was my name! Sister Elizabeth and I then moved on to the second nursery school, which was similar in construction and where the scenario with the apples was repeated.

Sister Elizabeth then escorted me to the primary school. Initially, we visited the classroom attended by students studying the first year's curriculum. It would be incorrect to say that all those present were in their first year of attendance. It is commonplace for students to repeat a year's study if they do not attain satisfactory results at the end of any year. During their time at primary school, a significant number of students repeat at least one year of their schooling. At this time, the classrooms contained very few desks. Most students sat on the floor. Desks that would accommodate two students in the United Kingdom often had three, four or sometimes five students squeezed into them. These classrooms could contain as many as sixty students. All students were obliged to wear a uniform of sorts. These uniforms were passed from student to student, so were often well worn, well patched and, more often than not, ill-fitting. Books were provided by the school, but the students were required to procure their own writing implements. Without exception, writing was in pencil. Pencils were sharpened at both ends to ensure maximum usage and minimum wastage, often not disposed of until grasping what remained of the pencil was a physical impossibility.

For many students, the advantage of attending school related to the food rather than the education. All attendees were entitled to a free lunch of maize in the middle of the day. For some, this was their only source of nourishment. The maize was distributed as a form of porridge and usually contained a small amount of sugar. It was cooked in a large cauldron over an open fire, the wood for which had to be gathered at a cost some distance from Loiyangalani.[7] Generating heat for cooking from solar power was to become a future project, once the Loiyangalani Trust had been established.

All lessons were conducted in a combination of Swahili and English with the latter becoming more prevalent as the students progressed through the system. It is worth noting that most of the children could speak three or even four languages even at a comparatively young age. They generally spoke their own tribal language at home, Swahili and English at school. Often, they could also converse in one or more of the other tribal languages. The atmosphere in the classrooms was electric. The enthusiasm for learning was immediately apparent. The concentration was intense. Education was key to any ambition to escape from the poverty that was all too apparent in the community, a fact that had obviously been impressed upon the children at a very young age. Conversing with the teachers, I realised too that helping the community necessitated maximising the educational opportunities for their children. I had been a teacher in England and overseas. It annoyed me that so many students in more affluent countries do not make the most of the opportunities offered by education. They do not have the aspirations of the Kenyan youngsters, who do what they can in very challenging circumstances. The classroom environment lacks so much of what we take for granted in our schools. I was to discover that the impetus to learn was generated by the women in the community. It was the women who wished to see the youngsters in the village extricated from a life of poverty and hopelessness.

I continued to distribute apples amongst the children, commencing with those in the lowest classes initially. Unfortunately, I did not have a sufficient quantity for the whole school, and it was the older pupils who missed out. It is interesting that many years later the distribution of the apples was remembered by the children. Perhaps I was destined to be for ever associated with apples!

I returned to the mission for lunch. The early afternoon was designated for rest and relaxation, which was most welcome. Having not managed to sleep well at night, I was tired. I returned to my quarters. Outside was a concrete path which was warm but shaded from the sun.

[7] See page 14.

There was a pleasant breeze, and I decided it was an ideal location for a short nap. It was not long before I was visited by Father Evarist. He was a little alarmed by my decision to make use of the path in this manner. Apparently, snakes also regard concrete paths as an ideal location to rest during the afternoon. I could soon be sharing my concrete path with a most unwelcome visitor! I decided that a confrontation with a snake of any description was not a good idea. Being bitten by a snake was not on my list of priorities. Once Father Evarist had retreated, I had somehow lost my enthusiasm for a siesta of any description, so I swam in the mission's swimming pool, where I was safe from any creature that might present itself.

In the late afternoon, I wandered into the main part of the village, where the huts were located. This is the area first observed by visitors approaching the village from the road along the lake. Most of the inhabitants are very poor and have little in the way of possessions. Generally, the huts are circular, which offers the most protection from the wind. Posts are dug into the ground to a depth of between twelve and fifteen centimetres, a substantial task given the terrain upon which these huts are erected. Reeds from palm trees are bound together to form the walls. A combination of reeds and old sacks is used to build the roof. As there is a complete ban on the use of any natural materials in the area, items for construction have to be gathered from elsewhere and carried to the village. This often entails a journey of between fifteen and twenty kilometres depending upon exactly what is required. The constant battering from the high winds necessitates frequent repairs. The contents of the huts are very basic. The families sleep on the ground on a sack if they are lucky, often sharing their accommodation with the ubiquitous scorpions.[8] On occasions the huts have an external compound in which members of the family can sit. These compounds may also be used for the accommodation of the odd goat or chicken. Chickens were scarce. Those that I did see were extremely skinny, giving the impression that survival was tough. It was truly humbling to realise that such basic accommodation was what these children and their families called home. They have little choice but to make the best of what they have. There are more substantial buildings owned by wealthier members of the community in the area where the school and mission are located.

---

[8] See page 126 for a more detailed description for the inside of a hut.

Undoubtedly, there is poverty in the United Kingdom, and it must be extremely difficult when families are compelled to prioritise the allocation of funds to ensure that the children receive the basic necessities of life. It should be pointed out, though, that these 'basic necessities' are relative to the situation in which we find ourselves. Poverty in Loiyangalani cannot begin to be compared with 'poverty' in the developed world. Those living in the United Kingdom often have no idea as to the hardships suffered by those trying to feed their children in some of the African countries. Being shown pictures of starving children on the television tugs at the heartstrings, and it is all too easy to be persuaded to part with cash in the belief that we can make a significant contribution to alleviate the situation. These funds provide, at best, only temporary relief. Once the donation has been made and the next show fills the television screen, the poverty is forgotten. Only by visiting these communities to experience first-hand the conditions under which the inhabitants survive does one fully appreciate the meaning of the word 'poverty'.

Upon visiting the area, I became the centre of attention. Word that 'A is for Apple' was approaching spread very quickly. Whether or not I was expected to produce more apples, I have no idea. The very young children were intrigued to hold a 'white' hand. Some of them were keen to inspect my skin, possibly thinking I had black skin underneath the white. The Kenyan adults do not have hair growing on the backs of their hands or their arms. I would not describe myself as hairy, but a limited amount of growth is evident. This hair was a source of amusement to the youngsters. There was a certain amount of stroking and even pulling of the hair to ascertain whether it was securely fixed to my skin. I very soon resembled the Pied Piper, with some children attached to my arms and others following close behind.

Sister Elizabeth accompanied me, guiding me to specific families where there was at least one family member who understood a modicum of English. I could then ask questions about their families and their lifestyle. They were very forthcoming with their responses. They had learnt to be content with what they had. In particular, I was impressed with the broad smiles on the faces of the younger children. There were no manufactured toys, as such. Any form of play required improvisation. The children are very happy to discover innovative ways to use any discarded item that they may chance upon. All 'toys' are fabricated by older family members from any scraps that can be procured. Cars have wheels fashioned from wire. Wheelbarrows are constructed from discarded plastic drums. Recycling is key to all these gadgets.

The clothes worn by the children had obviously been worn by many children before them. Some tops were branded with the names of sporting teams, mainly from America. One could imagine that once upon a time, these items had been the treasured possessions of wealthy children living on the other side of the world. Their cast-offs were these children's 'new' clothes. Other items of clothing bore the scars of many repairs and patches sewn on by loving mothers in an effort to prolong the life of the garments. The only 'smart' clothes were the school uniforms, but as mentioned previously, these often looked tired.

I observed children who were endeavouring to supplement the meagre income of their family by completing menial labour for a pittance. I watched a young boy and girl, probably brother and sister, both aged between about eight and eleven. They were sitting on the ground with a small pile of rocks, using one rock to crush other larger rocks. The crushed rocks could then be sold and used as building materials mainly for repairing the roads. A pile of rocks would sell for the equivalent of a few pence. The concept of a minimum wage was beyond the wildest dreams of anyone. Yes, we would regard it as the equivalent of slave labour or child exploitation, but the children involved cared only about creating a small source of valuable income to help provide food for their family. When a family starts with absolutely nothing, every single penny means so much to them. There is no 'universal credit' or any other type of benefit in Kenya. Every last penny has to be earnt. One has to experience the situation in order to appreciate exactly what they are attempting to do and why. It was distressing to watch these children, knowing that they performed this task day in and day out once they returned home after school. What a life!

Jacob has pointed out that many children are removed from school as they are required at home:

Child labour is common. Many children have dropped out of school to help their parents with their fishing or taking care of livestock. They sometimes stay home to help their grandparents, and some have to do household chores. It has been very common to have at least one child assigned by parents to take care of and help with grandparents. Elderly people require close attention, and this can mean the child being absent from school regularly, and in most cases the children do not come back again.

Once I had managed to extricate myself from my entourage of hangers-on, I walked to the top of the hillock and watched the sun disappear over the lake. This is always a surreal and beautiful experience, but how many of those living in the local community really appreciated it? Like so many of the daily events, this was a routine occurrence. To me, this was an example of beauty and joy amongst deprivation, but deprivation that contained an element of hope, hope that things would improve for the next generation.

On our way back to the mission, Sister Elizabeth took me to Benedict's house. I had met Benedict on my previous trip to Loiyangalani with Father Joya. He had driven us to Mount Kulal. He has since become a very good friend and it is worth pausing the narrative to relate his story.

Benedict was born in a small village called Halfare. Halfare is not far from Korr, which in turn is southwest of Marsabit. His parents were nomads. He spent the first years of his life wandering from place to place with his family, seeking suitable pasture for their livestock, mainly in the area between Baragoi and South Horr. When he was about eleven, the family decided to make their way north to Lake Turkana, as they had heard that the grazing was better in that area. Benedict belongs to the Rendille tribe. They had reached the shores of the lake when they were surrounded by a substantial group of young Turkana tribesmen armed with spears. It soon became obvious that they had their eyes on the family's livestock and were intent on killing each member of the family. Benedict recalls being convinced that his life would end at that very moment. It must have been truly terrifying for a young boy. It was the intervention of one of the older Turkana tribesmen that saved them. For some reason, he decided that as the family was travelling through the Turkana country, it did not present any threat to the locals, and so Benedict's family and stock were permitted to continue their journey unscathed. Benedict told me that he could not believe how lucky he and his family had been. Such was the nature of inter-tribal rivalry at the time that the slaughtering of members of neighbouring tribes in order to procure their livestock was a common occurrence. Benedict and his family arrived safely in the Lake Turkana region, and he was able to attend Loiyangalani Primary School for five years.

He managed to join the staff at the Oasis Lodge, first as a receptionist, then as a waiter. He was promoted to the post of assistant manager, receiving on-the-job training from the manager. After six years in this post, he left the Oasis Lodge and managed to establish his own business. Eventually, by 2000, he had accumulated sufficient funds to establish the Palm Shade Camp. Initially it was a campsite, but in 2004 he built the first of the traditional huts offering more permanent accommodation. Palm Shade Camp was used by the film company Blue Sky as its base for the production of the film *The Constant Gardener*. Since then, Benedict has expanded the site to include more substantial buildings. The camp is used regularly by organisations such as Médecins Sans Frontières. He is proud of the fact that he now employs twenty permanent staff and Palm Shade Camp has become the most popular place to stay in Loiyangalani. For someone who started life as a nomad and has only had five years of very basic education, Benedict's achievements have been considerable.

On this occasion, I had a discussion regarding the perpetual water supply. I was intrigued to understand how Mount Kulal could be the source of so much water. He explained that the level of the water within the mountain could easily be observed by visiting a spring high up in the mountain. Although the spring could not be accessed by vehicle, it was possible to reach it by climbing part of the mountain. This was like a red rag to a bull! I expressed an interest in seeing this spring, so Benedict said that we could go tomorrow. Little did I know quite what I was in for. Being a very naïve Englishman, I did make some very strange decisions without really considering the implications!

I had another interesting night in my sleeping quarters, but each night I was able to sleep more soundly as I began to realise that I was safe from the advances of the scorpions. In the morning, I had my usual breakfast; nothing extra to fortify me for my mountain adventure! I walk long distances in the United Kingdom on a regular basis, so the length of the walk was of no great concern to me. However, when participating in these events at home, I always ensure that there are adequate provisions for each expedition. Asking the Consolata Fathers to provide me with sufficient sustenance for this undertaking seemed to be beyond their comprehension. They had no idea what would be appropriate. It appeared that what they could give me would either disintegrate or melt in the heat. In the end I was presented with a few dried biscuits and a small water bottle, hardly an auspicious start to the expedition!

Benedict, together with two friends, drove me for about an hour along an old 'track' that did not appear to have been used for years. We halted at the mouth of one of the gorges, Laratchi, that forms part of Mount Kulal. Quite what Benedict and his friends thought about this crazy Englishman who wished to climb part of this mountain in the heat of the day, I dread to think! They were extremely patient. Initially, we made good progress. They chatted to themselves, and I strode out in front. At least there was a path of sorts. It was not long before I began to feel the effect of the heat. The path was thankfully shielded from the glare of the sun, but that did not mean that it was not hot. I had not appreciated just how energy-sapping the trek was to be. It was not long before I began to regret having decided to partake in the adventure. I do possess a certain amount of pig-headed determination. Having dragged Benedict and his friends out from Loiyangalani, I could not yield to my inner feelings, and so on we proceeded. Benedict had anticipated my need for extra water, so with my supply having been consumed, he was on hand to assist my rapidly developing thirst. He also assured me that there would be the opportunity to replenish our water supply later in the journey.

We reached a water hole to find a young lad watering his goats. I am unsure as to who was more surprised to see whom. I presume that he had seen a white man previously, but I am quite certain he had never expected to see one emerge from the path and frequent that particular water hole at that time of day! Benedict swiftly put him at ease. I decided that this oasis was an ideal opportunity to quench my thirst. Benedict immediately dampened my enthusiasm by pointing out that the water was unsafe to drink unless it could be filtered. It contained nasty parasites that could cause extreme sickness. The phrase by the poor seamen, marooned at sea – "Water, water everywhere and not a drop to drink" – immediately sprang to mind. I am, though, one of those old-fashioned people who still believe in linen handkerchiefs. No paper hankies for me! When I produced the handkerchief, it was deemed sufficiently proficient to be used as a filter so that I would live to see another day upon drinking the water. I have used these handkerchiefs for all sorts of tasks, but never for filtering water. This was the first and probably the last time it would be used in such a way.

Upon seeing this pool, I had begun to believe that perhaps we had reached our destination – but oh no! To reach the particular spring that we had decided to visit required a further climb. Benedict obviously knew the area well. The presence of the young lad with his goats indicated to me that we were probably travelling along a well-worn path used by the locals on a regular basis. Eventually, we reached an inauspicious spring where cool, clear water was bubbling to the surface and trickling down the hill. The distinct advantage to me was that the water could be drunk without requiring a handkerchief as a filter! This was indeed the spring that Benedict had wished to show me. He explained that this spring was the highest visible source of water within the mountain. The water stored in the mountain reached this level, possibly even higher, but there were no other visible outlets further up the mountain. If there was sufficient pressure for water to be bubbling out of the ground at this level, there must be a considerable volume of water stored within the bowels of the mountain. The water travelled from the foot of this 'reservoir' and emerged in Loiyangalani at the spring in the village.

We replenished our stocks. We had climbed to a significant height, but I was very relieved that the summit of the mountain was not our goal.[9] We then commenced our descent. I had anticipated this would be easier than the ascent, but that was not to be. I was rapidly succumbing to extreme thirst. I was also hungry, but endeavouring to consume dry biscuits when one's mouth is completely dry is an ordeal of its own. The descent was of necessity very slow, with several stops to rest weary limbs and summon sufficient energy to proceed. When we eventually sighted the vehicle at the end of track, a considerable sigh of relief was forthcoming, probably from Benedict and his friends as well! By this time the water had been drunk, so a speedy trip to Loiyangalani was hoped for. Alas, it was not to be. Twice the truck came to a grinding halt. On each occasion I had visions of being stranded in the middle of nowhere with no food and no water. One should never doubt the skills of the Kenyans. The problems were fixed, and we arrived in Loiyangalani safe and sound.

We had been away for seven hours. I must have looked shattered, because Sister Elizabeth expected me to be confined to bed for the whole of the next day. As it happened, once I had been fed and watered, particularly the latter, I was able to recover quite swiftly. It was not the distance walked but the heat that had been my problem. It had certainly been an experience to be remembered. At the time, I believed that I would not again be participating in expeditions on foot in the African heat! It

---

[9] See Chapter 9 ('An Unusual Christmas') on page 129 for a second experience of climbing this mountain.

appears that years later I had forgotten about the travails of expeditions in the heat, because on a much later trip I was to climb an interesting hill that nearly defeated me for similar reasons.[10]

Sister Elizabeth was pleasantly surprised when I emerged apparently unscathed for Mass on the following morning, having been convinced that I would be suffering from yesterday's ordeal. As before, the service lasted most of the morning. Yet again, I was a person of interest. My presence was acknowledged with smiles and giggles from some of the younger children. I seemed to hear "A is for Apple" all over the place. There was little else planned for the day, so I spent the afternoon with Benedict and his family.

The following day was spent in the village. I had another interesting conversation with the headmaster. I was able to observe the pupils having their lunch. For many, they had had very little to eat since Friday. It was noticeable that once they had eaten, they were more susceptible to learning. I made a mental note that offering breakfast rather than lunch might be a more useful way of utilising the resources. Ideally, they should have both, but learning in the morning would be more productive on full rather than empty stomachs.

Sister Elizabeth and I then returned to the El Molo village. She again endeavoured to persuade the women to part with their wares before receiving full payment, but to no avail. I have no idea whether they were eventually to discover the considerable sums of money that the women in Loiyangalani were to amass simply because they were to trust me, but the El Molo women turned down the opportunity that was presented to them first. We said our farewells. Father Evarist then took us to the two springs that are used for medicinal purposes. The first of these has a foul odour, and I was instructed not to taste the water. The second spring was very different, and I was permitted to sample the water, which had a sweet taste. Sister Elizabeth explained how the springs combined to produce healing. The cure was primarily for upset stomachs. Drinking from the first spring induced violent vomiting. Drinking from the second one then settled the stomach. I commented that it seemed a rather drastic and undignified approach to curing the ailment, but apparently it worked. Fortunately, not succumbing to any such ailments during any of my visits, I never had the need to resort to discovering whether, in fact, this form of medication was indeed the success that it purported to be!

[10] See page 146.

I was then dropped off at the Daballens' hut. Magdalen and her mother had expressed a wish that I visit before returning south. They were again very appreciative of what I had done. Thankfully, there were no invitations to dine this time. It would have been a great pity if they had sacrificed another goat on my behalf. I did discover that Laura's husband, as a young man, had been in the first expedition to circumnavigate Lake Turkana.

I was chaperoned by Sister Elizabeth on my final day in the village. She took me to the dispensary, a rather elaborate name for the health centre. This had originally been established by the Consolata mission. At this stage, it was run entirely by the Sisters. I never discovered exactly what training was required in order to become a Sister in one of these outposts, but it seemed to me that they had to be adept as nursery school teachers and have a basic knowledge of nursing, which included the administration of certain drugs. The nearest hospital, at Wamba, was too far to be of any use in a real emergency. The Sisters were required to cater for any complications with pregnancies and births, malaria (not common, fortunately), snake and scorpion bites, bronchitis, heat rashes and boils. All medical provisions were trucked from Nairobi. As transport can be most unreliable, it was not unknown for medicine to arrive that was past its 'use by' date. Although the Sisters did all they could to ensure the premises were cleaned regularly, there was the inevitable lack of sanitisation. The walls of the building were crumbling. The wind ensured that dust seeped in through any orifices. There must have been times when the Sisters were overwhelmed by the situation presented to them by their patients. Knowing that an efficient hospital could have saved lives that they were unable to save must have been extremely frustrating.

I had been intrigued by another mission in the area that had been established by an American organisation, so I parted company with Elizabeth briefly in order to visit it. These missionaries and their families lived in a well-fortified compound which boasted of its own guard day and night. I was to discover that although they shared the same Christian beliefs as the Consolata mission, they operated in a very different way. My first introduction to them had been the sight of an American teenager proceeding at great speed towards the village on a quad bike, doubtless to procure something from a local store. I approached the compound and had to wait while the security guard asked the incumbents whether they were willing to allow me to enter. Upon receiving a positive response, I ventured into their living quarters. It was akin to being transported to some metropolis far away from Loiyangalani.

There were two families in residence. The children, who each had their own computer, were either playing games or participating in education direct from America. The amenities were incredible; no expense had been spared. The rooms appeared to have had some type of air conditioning. The bulk of their food had been purchased either from Marsabit or possibly Nairobi. They did not seem to want for anything. It was certainly a mini oasis in the middle of nowhere. A church had been established for the local inhabitants as an alternative to the Catholic church. Apparently, there was a small congregation comprising principally of villagers who lived near their church. Apart from conducting the church services, their interaction with the community seemed to be minimal. At no stage did they offer assistance at the dispensary or the schools. To me, their presence raised more questions than it answered, but they, and the mission who financed them, believed they were satisfying a need and providing alternative Christian worship. I imagine that few, if any, of the locals had entered their premises, so possibly they were unaware of the disparity between the lifestyle of these missionaries and that of themselves. I had thought the Consolata Missionaries were living a life of luxury when compared with their congregation, but that was before I had made this visit. In their defence, they had young families, the members of which required certain necessities if they were to ensure that they could be raised and educated to meet the expectations of their peers in America. Gone were the days when missionaries and their families had very little in the way of home comforts.

My final afternoon was spent at what turned out to be a crucial meeting with a local women's group in Loiyangalani. Sister Elizabeth had managed to convince them to trust me with their goods. She had somehow persuaded them that the taboo concerning the releasing of wares without prior payment should be abandoned. The group was making necklaces, bracelets and little animals that would slide on to key rings. As the items were comparatively small, I was able to acquire a reasonable amount without overburdening my luggage allowance. Entrusting me with the items without receiving any cash was obviously quite a leap of faith for them. Fortunately, Sister Elizabeth was highly regarded, and they entrusted me with the items, despite in all probability initially harbouring thoughts that they might never see the fruits of their labours. As it turned out, it was a decision that for a few years was to benefit them financially in a way that they could never have imagined. It was also a feather in my cap. Yes, they had seen me with Father Joya on my previous visit and they knew that I had helped fund the education of more than one student, but I could have been unscrupulous and retained all proceeds from the sales of the items for myself. Mind you, that would have been the final nail in any coffin regarding future trips to Loiyangalani!

I had one further night in which to do battle with the shower and attempt to receive a modicum of sleep under very trying circumstances. I cannot say that I was unhappy to leave my quarters for the last time on the next day. Fortunately, my accommodation in Loiyangalani was to be of a higher standard on all future visits. I was to find out on a later visit that it was very rare for visitors to sleep in the quarters to which I had been assigned, unless there was a surplus of lodgers. I never did discover why it had been decided that I should sample its delights!

After breakfast, Father Evarist drove Sister Elizabeth and me to Baragoi. We were accompanied by a mother and her sick child who needed to receive attention at Wamba Hospital. I had been asked to provide the necessary funds for the operation and any additional expenses that might be incurred. I knew very little about Wamba Hospital, but it was the only significant hospital for miles around. Jacob has a story to tell about a group of people who were to receive treatment here:

On one occasion, a generous gift by friends of Professor Meissel was used to help some of the El Molo people receive treatment for their eyes. One of the patients, Marko Lekorsinte, from the village near the primary school, could see nothing and was on the list to be treated at Wamba hospital. A few days before the journey to Wamba, he told me that we had to give the opportunity for treatment to someone else, as he needed to be present at his eldest son's wedding. I tried to convince him that he should push the traditional wedding to a later date as currently he could not see his son's new wife or enjoy the wedding. Once he had got his sight back, he would be able to see everyone and take a bigger part in the wedding. He agreed and therefore asked his son to postpone the wedding to a later date. He went for treatment and regained his sight, so he was happily able to oversee his son's wedding.

Father Evarist had decided that he wished to do the return journey in one day. The vehicle was pushed to its limits, and I did wonder how we reached our destination without so much as a puncture. Suffice it to say, there was a considerable amount of bouncing around in the rear of the vehicle, which had become my customary position for many of these early journeys in the vehicles. Due to the rapidity of our progress, we arrived in Baragoi ahead of schedule, so once Father Evarist had made his departure, there was time to relax before lunch.

After lunch Sister Elizabeth, the women, her sick child and I boarded a *matatu* to transport us to Maralal. The owners of these vehicles endeavour to accommodate as many passengers as possible in order to maximise their earnings. Seating capacity is regularly ignored, so passengers resemble sardines in a can. Sufficiency of leg room and other such luxuries can only be dreamt about. The route to one's destination is inevitably circuitous. There is always the need to entice more passengers aboard, especially should anyone wish to alight at an intermediate location between designated stops. The four of us were joined by seven other passengers, so managing to extricate oneself hastily in the event of an emergency was most unlikely should the need arise, a sobering thought!

There is a direct route from Baragoi to Maralal which is marked on all maps. There is another longer route via Barsaloi which often fails to figure on maps. No prizes for guessing which we were destined to take! I think we probably shed one passenger and gained another by following this route. The view from our privileged positions was limited to say the least. A very steep climb into Maralal was interesting, as we were seated on what could best be described as benches facing sideways. The unfortunate individual on either side at the rear of the vehicle was compelled to accommodate the weight of his fellow passengers sliding towards him. Upon arrival at our destination, I managed to disembark, but only once I had persuaded various parts of my body that they should commence functioning again, which resulted in me landing in a heap on the ground. It required more than one 'soda'[11] to revive me and give me enough strength to board a vehicle that had been provided to ferry Sister Elizabeth and me to the mission. We made provisions to ensure that the woman and her child would reach Wamba safely, and so we parted company from them at this point. I assumed that I would never encounter

[11] cool fizzy drink

them again, an assumption that was to be proved wrong seventeen years later! I was pleased to have an opportunity to recover from the discomforts of the journey once we were safely ensconced in the mission. Little did I know that my ordeal was far from over.

Maralal would always be remembered for my battles with the mosquitoes, and on this occasion it was no different! Sister Elizabeth and I did have to arise at 5.15 am, so breakfast was also very early. We were then driven back into the town centre so that we could resume our journey! We boarded another *matatu* to continue our journey south. Despite there being twelve passengers, according to my diary, I had the luxury of sufficient leg room to travel in a modicum of comfort. We travelled to Nyahururu, where we were deposited and instructed to find another vehicle for the remainder of the journey.

We could now experience the joy of a standard *matatu*! From here on, the road was tarmac. These *matatus* are small minibuses resembling the old Kombi vans in size and shape. The rear of the vehicle is filled with as many seats as possible. Seemingly, passengers are midgets or legless human beings requiring little or no leg room. If I had been uncomfortable in the first of the two previous vehicles, that was a mild inconvenience compared with the discomfort I was about to experience. I am tall, and the distance between my seat and the one in front was such that my body could only be described as being in a vertical foetal position! *Matatus* are usually brightly coloured, travelling with music blaring, so that their presence could not be ignored. Fortunately, the music was usually confined to *matatus* in Nairobi. The vehicles stop at the behest of any prospective passenger, not necessarily at a designated stopping place. Generally, they are operated by two people, one driving and one collecting fares. The latter is liable to leap off at any point in a town where possible passengers may linger, in the hope of persuading some unsuspecting person that his *matatu* is the most desirable mode of transport to the next destination.

Restrictions have tightened over the years, so much so that *matatus* are expected to stop only at designated stops, but this was not the case at that time. My desire was to reach journey's end as soon as possible, but whenever the vehicle had vacant seats, we crawled at a snail's pace in the hope of attracting custom, something I found most frustrating. It was also not unheard of to have additional passengers clinging to various parts of the exterior of the vehicle, but again this usually only happened on shorter journeys. There have been horrendous accidents over the years involving these vehicles. It is obvious that a swift exit from the vehicle in an emergency would be impossible. Very few tourists, apart from the young and brave, ever use them, so I was taking quite a risk. The driving is usually horrendous, with a mad dash at great speed between towns and the incessant crawling within the towns. Timetables do not exist, so departure and arrival times were dependent entirely upon the whim of the driver. There were no refreshment stops or comfort breaks. Once ensconced, one was *in situ* until one decided to disembark. Another frustrating factor on this journey was the need to detour in order to deposit passengers and collect additional ones in towns that would not normally feature on the route. To say I was relieved and pleased to reach our destination in the middle of Nairobi was an understatement. Disentangling myself from my seat required a superhuman effort. Sister Elizabeth and I then used a taxi to reach the seminary in time for a late lunch. In many ways, I was happy to be able to say that I had managed to travel in two forms of *matatu* and survived to tell the tale, an experience I have thankfully not had to repeat since.

After lunch, I said farewell to Sister Elizabeth, and we parted company. As it happened, it was the last time that I was to see her, although we did continue to communicate by mail for a while. The Consolata Sisters, like the Fathers, are posted to communities for short stints, so are continually on the move. She had been a wonderful chaperone and had enabled me to experience Loiyangalani to the full. Her endeavours regarding the women and their wares would bear fruit to a greater extent than she could ever have envisaged. She had been a very positive encouragement to the women in Loiyangalani in many ways, chiefly by persuading them to initiate projects that could assist them in earning money and improving their standard of living.

This was the end of the trip and I returned to England the next day. It had been an interesting experience but had ignited in me a desire to help the community in Loiyangalani as much as possible.

CHAPTER FIVE

Consolidating Ideas

My next trip to Loiyangalani was in February 2009. I had managed modest achievements since my previous visit, Magdalene was close to becoming a fully qualified nurse, and I was looking to sponsor another student. The selling of the artefacts that the women had given me had been a great success. Additional items had arrived either transported by friends travelling to and from Kenya or, on one occasion, shipped across. Stock control was the major issue. Money was sent to the women via the Consolata mission and various other intermediaries, but the women were no doubt not only pleased but also very relieved that their trust in me had reaped dividends. Being relatively cheap, the items appealed to youngsters at various fetes and shows, so were not difficult to sell.

I again travelled to Kenya on my own. I was fortunate to be met by Father Joya. Once I had had some time to relax after my flight, he kindly took me into Nairobi. Parking was no easier than last time. I was slightly alarmed when he double parked in a particular car park. These car parks are watched over by security staff, so the precise spot where we left the car was chosen after some negotiation. I could only assume that it had been decided that the owner of the car that we had blockaded would be in no hurry to depart, given that extrication would have necessitated a pair of wings.

The main objective of the visit to the city was to cash some of my traveller's cheques that I had acquired in England. As with previous trips, I had been advised that this was the safest way to convey money. As Barclays Bank has branches in Nairobi, I had always purchased their traveller's cheques. On my previous visits, exchanging them had been a relatively painless operation, although obtaining the optimum exchange rate could be a challenge. It is not difficult to imagine my sense of horror when the branch of Barclays that I had chosen to visit in Nairobi not only refused to exchange the traveller's cheques but made it quite clear that I would have difficulty exchanging them at any bank, Barclays or otherwise, not only in Nairobi but in the whole of Kenya! No amount of cajoling or pleading could persuade them to cooperate. It was explained to me that the reason for the non-acceptance of traveller's cheques related to the ease with which they could be reproduced and used fraudulently. I did indeed try other banks, but was met with the same response. My traveller's cheques were useless and could only be redeemed upon my return to England. What a shambles! I could not understand why banks did not appear to communicate with each other between countries, especially being the same bank. Why had somebody in England not been able to inform me that the traveller's cheques were useless in Kenya?

With poor Father Joya having to accompany me from bank to bank, I had to return to the original Barclays Bank and arrange to withdraw cash. Fortunately, the bank was more than happy to facilitate the transaction, but not only did this place severe pressure on my cash reserves, as I had exchanged a fair amount for the traveller's cheques, but it also required me to carry around more cash than I perceived to be safe.

I purchased some beads for the ladies for the construction of more beaded artefacts. Helping them financially was one reason behind this purchase but choice of the colours of the individual beads was another.[12] I was amazed that it is not possible to purchase purple beads. At that time, the beads were imported from the Czech Republic, so I could not understand why purple should be an undesirable colour, but no, the original supplier did not make purple beads. Extraordinary! Shopping and money matters completed, we returned to the car; fortunately, with no sign of a frustrated owner of the car which we had blockaded waiting to berate us!

Next stop was the greengrocer for yet more apples! Whether it was the same that we had visited last time, I have no idea, but he was pleasantly surprised to be able to fulfil my order for three boxes of apples. I had decided that due to the success of these pieces of fruit on my last visit, I would repeat the exercise.

It was the following day that my journey north commenced. Father Evarist had been replaced by Father Andrew and an assistant, Father Fabio, who had arrived recently from his native South America. I am not

[12] See page 78.

sure why the Consolata Order needed to recruit priests from there, but he seemed happy to have been posted to Kenya. It was he who was to be my designated driver for the trip to Loiyangalani. Unfortunately, his driving prowess was very similar to that of the Kenyans. We dawdled through Nairobi at a snail's pace. He seemed convinced that every other vehicle on the road was a potential source of disaster and should be approached with the maximum of caution. I was permitted to sit in the front of the vehicle, even though we had a Consolata Sister as an additional passenger, accompanying us as far as Maralal, also sitting in the front. She was not the most petite of the Consolata Sisters, and so space was again at a premium. At least by sitting in the front, my view of the countryside through which we were passing improved considerably. At one stage, we halted to procure a sack of potatoes from a vendor selling his wares at the side of the road. Although shops exist in the towns and villages, there is no shortage of hopefuls endeavouring to sell produce at the side of the road. Trading licences do not appear to be a necessity in Kenya. In fact, there are so many roadside vendors that one wonders exactly how much they manage to sell on any given day. Many cannot make more than a few shillings (the local currency is the Kenyan Shilling) each day. Sadly, poverty is never far away.

We stopped in Nyakururu. Father Fabio had been given a list of purchases to be made and had, for some reason, chosen this village to be his source of the goods. Supermarkets do not exist in these places. The stores each specialise in different items, rather as villages in England used to many years ago. It was amusing to note that stores selling meat of any description are called a 'butchery'. Hopefully, the actual butchery does not take place in the store, but perhaps it does, who knows? We entered what was the 'general' store. It resembled something similar to Ronnie Barker's store in *Open All Hours*, the main difference being the presence of a considerable amount of dust that had settled on many of the items. Perhaps this is a polite way of describing the residue that lay on certain products. Casting a beady eye around, I did wonder how long some of the items had been *in situ*. 'Use by' dates are non-existent. Some of the less popular items had probably been nestling in their abodes for a considerable length of time, waiting to be handed over to some unsuspecting customer. I have often wondered about the need for these 'use by' dates on many items in the United Kingdom. Surely, we possess sufficient intelligence to determine whether something is fit for consumption? Yes, we should be careful with perishable items, but I have often eaten fruit and vegetables that have professed to be past their 'use by' date. I am not Einstein, but I do possess sufficient intelligence to ascertain whether most items can be consumed without consequently necessitating a hasty trip to the little boys' room or, worse, the local hospital, or whether they should be confined to the bin. I digress!

Suffice it to say, those who purchase the items in these stores do not appear to suffer from food poisoning. The customers continue to return day after day. It is also fortunate that, as yet, Kenya does not suffer from a 'blame culture' in which every accident or mishap is somehow attributable directly to an individual or a company and therefore presents the opportunity for some unscrupulous lawyer to litigate and sue the unfortunate party. Accidents and illnesses in Kenya are usually attributed to bad luck or being acts of God, the latter being rather difficult to sue!

Having completed his purchases, Father Fabio decided it was time to resume the journey north. Again, as with the Kenyan drivers, Father Fabio's driving habits seemed to change once the tarmac ceased, instead to be replaced by dirt. Granted, there were fewer vehicles to be regarded as potential sources of any accident, but the dirt seemed to give him the licence to apply more pressure to the accelerator than perhaps I would have done in similar circumstances. He also appeared to have an aversion to being overtaken by another vehicle along this road. I pondered the situation, attributing it to a possible unfulfilled youthful desire to be a rally driver. Later I was to discover that the reasons were, in fact, more sinister!

Although we arrived in Maralal after dark, there was again more shopping to complete. I did think this strange. Why could the shopping not wait until the morning? I never managed to discover what constituted the opening and closing times of the shops. The proprietors of these establishments were so willing to trade that they would probably not have been averse to being hauled out of bed in the middle of the night in order to satisfy the needs of a particular customer! Shops did appear to remain open for excessive stretches of time.

We stayed overnight at the mission in Maralal. A bishop was in attendance and entertained me with interesting stories of his life in Kenya. My accommodation seemed to have been slightly upgraded since my previous visit. Unfortunately, the mosquitoes were still in attendance and seemed to have been eagerly awaiting my return with the sole aim of discovering how much of a disruption they could be to my night's abode. Despite my usual defences with the towel, it was to be another losing battle. I did manage some sleep, but the combination of the mosquitos and the heat ensured it was a long night.

Father Fabio had informed me that he wished to depart very early in the morning, leaving before breakfast. I was therefore up at 5 am, not particularly difficult given my encounter with the mosquitos! Yet again, we had exchanged vehicles for the journey north. We also no longer had any passengers. The road north of Maralal was only deemed drivable in the more capable four-wheel-drive vehicles, as the roads were horrendous in places. We departed while most of the town continued to slumber. I was surprised when we found ourselves on the road that leads to Baragoi via Barsaloi. It was a less direct route, and the condition of the road was far worse than that of the normal one. In fact, this was the route we had used on my previous return trip in the infamous *matatu*. On that occasion it had been necessary due to the need to deposit one of the passengers in Barsaloi. There was no such need on this occasion. The descent from Maralal along this route was horrendous. Endeavouring to spot the various hazards in the road, which was riddled with large and often deep potholes, was a challenge. Eventually, the sun rose, the descent ceased and the road improved. We stopped at a very remote missionary outpost south of Barsaloi, where we were treated to breakfast. It was only then that Father Fabio could reveal the explanation for his slightly erratic driving yesterday evening and the reasons for the hasty departure this morning using what is generally termed "the back road".

Father Fabio commenced by pointing to two holes in the door on my side of the vehicle, which resembled bullet holes and which, as it was dark when we had departed, I had failed to notice. Indeed, they *were* bullet holes! Joy of joy! On a recent journey, the vehicle had been fired at by bandits! Luckily for the passenger on that occasion, those firing would not have won any Olympic medals for shooting!

Father Fabio explained that yesterday he had been driving in such a way as to remain close to other vehicles on the road. There is safety in numbers, as bandits will rarely attack a vehicle if there is another vehicle in the vicinity. The early departure this morning via the back road was to avoid the possibility of being ambushed. Apparently, the advent of mobile phones had been a bonus for the activities of the bandits. 'Scouts' in the local towns phoned their fellow conspirators who had taken up residence further along the road, alerting them to the fact that an appropriate vehicle was about to depart laden with unsuspecting occupants and ripe for a lucrative ambush. Naturally, I was extremely glad not to have been forewarned of this subterfuge. Had I possessed any knowledge as to what might have been awaiting me, the mosquitos of the night before would have been the least of my worries when attempting to obtain a reasonable night's sleep. I was also relieved to discover that the danger had now ceased, as the bandits only operated within a limited area north and south of Maralal.

After breakfast, we embarked on the journey north through Baragoi and on to South Horr. I had time to observe the limited variety of wildlife that made their homes in this very arid country. The scenery was spectacular, but only due to the nature of the desolation of this wilderness. It was not hard to appreciate how difficult survival must be in these hot, arid, dusty conditions.

We did have one unexpected incident along the way. At one stage, an ostrich followed by six young chicks ran across the road in front of the vehicle. As we approached them, instead of planting his foot on the brake to ensure they had a safe crossing, Father Fabio planted it on the accelerator to ensure that he could run over as many of the chicks as possible! With a grin on his face, he announced that he had just procured supper! Three dead ostrich chicks were then deposited in the rear of our vehicle to be attended to later. It was pointless displaying any sense of horror. The incident further served to highlight the stark realities of living in Kenya. Any living creature that could be regarded as a possible meal is fair game. Although thankfully attitudes differ in the United Kingdom, it has been known for motorists happily to run over a pheasant and then secrete it into the back of the car, providing that the incident was not observed by other motorists.

We were served fruit for lunch at the mission in South Horr. The journey to Loiyangalani was interrupted by a short stay at a settlement, Sarima, which appeared to be in the middle of nowhere. I am not quite certain why we stopped, but Father Fabio seemed to know the locals and we were treated to a cup of *chi*, which is Swahili for 'tea'. It contained some milk, but I refrained from enquiring as to the source of the milk. It was probably best not to know, given that the only animals in the area were goats for whom cleanliness of any description was not a priority! The settlement had a stockade built around the perimeter as a defence against the possible intrusion of wild animals, who seemed to take great delight in sampling their goats. I didn't establish the nature of these predators, but I was to discover on a subsequent trip that lions do appear to frequent the area.

We continued to Loiyangalani. I was able to appreciate the fabulous view of Lake Turkana as one reaches the summit of the escarpment. It is a vista which one always appreciates. As the lake sparkles in the sunshine, there is this wonderful sense of peace and tranquillity.

Once in Loiyangalani, I was introduced to Father Andrew, a Kenyan, who had taken over from Father Evarist. On this occasion, I was permitted to use a room within the main building, as I had when accompanied by Father Joya. No banishment to the outbuildings, no battles with any undesirable creepy crawlies!

After what must have been a reasonable night's sleep, I emerged for breakfast and decided upon a quiet commencement to my visit. I wandered over to the primary school, where I was introduced to the new headmaster, Bosco; he was to become a key figure regarding my achievements in Loiyangalani. He was genuinely interested in ensuring that whatever I was to do in the future would maximise the needs of his students. He was very supportive of my efforts and was to be a very good host on my future visits. We discussed the immediate needs of the school, where desks were an obvious priority as large numbers of students were sitting on the floor in the classrooms.

My first task was to distribute the apples! As soon as a box appeared in a classroom, the eyes of the youngsters lit up. They had remembered them from my previous visit and there was no hesitation in taking the first bite! Having now produced apples on two occasions, this remained for many of the youngsters their earliest recollection regarding my presence.

Once the children were having their break, I was introduced to the other teachers, and we had an impromptu staff meeting so that the teachers could suggest ways in which I could assist. The need for equipment such as stationery and other teaching materials came as no surprise. One of the female teachers then came up with a suggestion that I had not anticipated: sanitary towels. For most of the girls, sanitary towels were a luxury they could not afford, so they were forced to remain at home when having their periods. Not only did they miss a significant quantity of classroom teaching, but they were also at times prevented from sitting their exams. When girls have their periods, they opt out of school and remain at home and may end up dropping out of school for good. Their parents cannot afford food, so no one can prioritise sanitary towels.

I took this request on board, not only on this visit, but in the future sanitary towels were to become a priority item once the Loiyangalani Trust was established. There is no doubt that this suggestion has transformed the lives of many of the girls who were to attend the school. If it had not been for the courage of this female teacher to come forward with what was undoubtedly an unusual suggestion in a male-dominated environment, it could have been some time before I, or anyone else from the charity, realised the enormity of the issue.

In this male-dominated society, it was the needs of the boys that were prioritised over those of the girls. Little changes, no matter which country is being discussed! Thankfully, there were to be improvements in the education of the girls. Over the years that I have been involved in Loiyangalani, women have become increasingly vocal in what should happen in the village. It was a privilege to be able to respond to the request for sanitary towels. Unfortunately, this particular teacher became ill and died soon after my visit. She was never able to appreciate the results of her suggestion. It is worth remembering that due to the fact that students often commence their education later than they do in England, combined with the fact that years are repeated, it is not unusual to see girls of sixteen or seventeen in the primary school. The constant flow of sanitary towels has now ensured that female students have continuous access to education.

After lunch I was given a tour of the secondary school. This had been constructed from funds raised by a very well-meaning group of people. They had even appointed an individual to oversee the task on their behalf. Unfortunately, the resources had been misused, so the buildings were incomplete. I had, in fact, met the initiators of the project while in England and had advised them against building the school. To me, this was another example of a group of people wishing to give something to the community without adequate planning and consideration as to how to most benefit those they wished to assist.

There were two issues. Implementation of a project such as the building of a school needs someone on the ground who is both accountable and trustworthy. Directing operations from England is impossible, and the individual chosen to oversee the project in Loiyangalani was not up to the task for whatever reason. I had been assured that more than sufficient money had been raised to fund the project, and yet apparently the money had disappeared before the completion of the buildings. Lack of thorough accounting had ensured that it was difficult to identify the exact nature of any possible misappropriation of the funds.

The second issue concerned the basic need for the secondary school. Students from Loiyangalani have always attended schools in the neighbouring towns and villages such as South Horr, Marsabit and Wamba. They board at these schools, as do most, if not all, of their fellow pupils from other towns and villages. The idea behind the building of a secondary school in Loiyangalani could appear very logical, as students could remain with their families instead of travelling vast distances for their education. Travel is expensive. Unfortunately, simply providing buildings for a new school does not solve the problem. Teachers and resources are required. In order for the school to become attractive to students, there is the need to ensure that high-achieving students attend. As the well-established schools have very high reputations, the students with potential will continue to attend these schools as the opportunity to maximise their achievement is greatest. They are naturally loath to possibly jeopardise their potential by attending an untried establishment. I spoke to the bright students who were about to leave the primary school. It soon became clear that they would rather board at one of the established schools than attend the secondary school in Loiyangalani. Also, being a new school and very remote, it was difficult to attract inspirational teachers. As a result, the Loiyangalani secondary school was understaffed, obtained poor results and was only attended by those whose grades were insufficiently high to permit entry into the established schools. It takes more than new buildings, especially incomplete ones, to change the habits of a community. The school was to continue to struggle for years to come, even when buildings were finally completed.

Implementing a project such as the building of a new school requires the support of the whole community. It requires someone *in situ* who is reliable and accountable. I have been very fortunate in having two such individuals over the years that I have been involved in Loiyangalani. Any project must also be sustainable. When it is completed, there must be a strategy to ensure that the objectives are met and maintained. It is sad that so many good intentions lead to the wanton expenditure of resources with little or nothing to show for the effort.

On my way back to the mission, I watched a game of soccer that was in progress. Using a football, as we know it, was out of the question. The rocky surface and the thorn bushes in the vicinity of the 'pitch' precluded the use of anything that was not extremely durable. The 'football' had been constructed from plastic bags that had been bound together using tape to represent an object that could be roughly described as spherical. Children of all ages appeared to be participating, some more actively than others. It was very much male-dominated, but it was pleasing to see one or two girls offering limited participation. On the whole, footwear was not mandatory, which served to demonstrate the toughness of the feet of these youngsters. Walking barefoot over the terrain would have been agonising in the extreme for most people, let alone running across it as these children were happily doing. There appeared to be no limit to the number of participants. There were no officials or referees, but the game seemed to flow and be played in good spirit. Diving in order to attract a free kick was out of the question. Not only would it have gone unnoticed, but it would also have been extremely painful! Cooperation and resourcefulness were there for all to see.

The following day, I met with the group of women whose wares I had been selling in England. A few problems had emerged. Colours admired by Kenyans did not necessarily match those preferred by the young girls in England purchasing, in particular the bracelets. Kenyans favour red and the darker colours. In England, no matter what one tries to say about sexism, there is no doubt that the favourite colour amongst the majority of young girls is pink. I am fully aware that one should not categorise sexes regarding colour preference, but I have sold sufficient numbers of bracelets at enough different locations to be able to state that, on the whole, young girls do prefer pink. Initially, I had had no pink bracelets to sell and had been asked why. It was only on this visit, when discussing colours with the women, that I was told that Kenyans detest pink as a colour. Persuading them that they had to use pink beads was no easy matter. As with anything that one creates, one is prone to use colours that one likes rather than those which one does not like! As I had purchased some pink beads which I gave to the women, they assured me that they would use them. Another problem concerned the size of the bracelets. The women did not have access to elastic, using nylon fishing line instead, so there was limited pliability in the bracelets. Little attention had been given to size, so the bracelets tended to be of one size. As the women were accustomed to making them for adults, we had to discuss the fact that smaller bracelets should be constructed.

I had also sold the little animals that they made as keyrings. The variety of animals had been rather limited to crocodiles and scorpions, as they were most common in the area. After a short discussion, they assured me they could make elephants and zebras, both of which were to be very popular. It was interesting broaching the idea of stock control with women who had never really had cause to consider any directives regarding what they were making. It was, though, the use of the pink beads that caused the most hilarity amongst the women. They could not understand why any individual could be seen wearing a necklace or bracelet with pink beads as part of its construction.

The women had seen the fruits of their labours in the past, so they assured me they would do what they could to ensure I had what I needed to continue the successful selling of the items. I observed them for a while. The skill that they demonstrated in constructing the little animals was incredible, threading the nylon fishing line through the tiny holes in the beads. They had magnificent eyesight and superb concentration. It was very sad that apart from me and a few tourists, the scope for selling their wares was very limited.

My next port of call was Laura's house. Magdalene was away finishing her course at nursing college in Wamba. Her mother, Laura, was again very pleased to see me. Refreshments were limited to *chi*, for which I was most grateful. I was relieved that there was no feast at which I would have to be a rather reluctant participant.

The highlight of the next day was the meeting with Albert. It was this meeting that was directly responsible for the establishment of the Loiyangalani Trust. I had told Bosco that I was looking to sponsor another of the students, as Magdalene's studies were nearing completion. Albert had achieved an excellent grade at the primary school, finishing top of his year. His family could not afford the fees to send him to any secondary school, as they were very poor nomads caring for a small flock of goats in the desert beyond the village. Albert was staying in a hut with his uncle, uncertain as to his future prospects. I was greatly impressed that despite such an uncertain future, Albert had decided to work hard at primary school to achieve so good a grade. I was very loath to describe myself as a 'knight in shining armour' (I have never been a knight, let alone in shining armour!), but there was no doubt that as far as Albert was concerned, I had appeared in the right place at the right time. In his eyes, it was God who had performed this miracle. I was happy with that, provided that I was not confused with God! Because the school term had commenced and I did not have the cash (only useless travellers' cheques!) with me to facilitate entrance into the one of the more prestigious secondary schools, it was decided he should attend Loiyangalani Secondary School.

I had my doubts as to the wisdom of this, but he wished to remain relatively close to his family, and so the arrangement suited him. Communication with the headmaster was initiated immediately. He was content for me to send the money for Albert's fees when I returned to England. I was to learn that sponsorship of students, even if money was not immediately forthcoming, was extremely desirable at any of the schools, as often money from local families was not as easy to extricate from the parents as the headmasters would have liked!

It was the fact that I was about to embark on a new sponsorship that could stretch beyond secondary school to an expensive university that led me to contemplate the establishment of a charity. I had been unable to claim gift aid on any of the money I had provided for Magdalene. By funnelling the donations through a charity, reclaiming the gift aid would bolster the balance available to support Albert, reducing the amount that I needed to find. I decided upon my return to England I would become the founder of a very small charity, so that I could reclaim this gift aid. Little did I realise at the time exactly where that decision would lead. In fact, the achievements of the charity have exceeded more than I could ever have dreamt. Channelling my funds through a charity would also mean that surplus funds could be used to offer support to the village in other ways. I did not offer any further suggestions at this stage, as I was wary of becoming overcommitted. I was genuinely delighted to be able to assist a young man who was obviously hard-working, intelligent but from a family who lacked the financial wherewithal to pursue the dreams of their son. This was actually to become a blueprint for determining which students to support when the charity began to expand.

My next visit was to the house of Benedict, whose achievements I discussed in chapter 4. He had had the foresight to realise that tourism was on the increase. Loiyangalani had The Lodge and a campsite, but there was the need for something that could be described as more 'middle of the road'. As mentioned previously, Benedict initially started with six huts, but as the number of visitors increased, so did his facilities. His camp has a communal eating area with food provided by a cook and other staff. Benedict's family also experienced another stroke of luck. One of his daughters, upon completion of her secondary education, had been singled out as the recipient of a scholarship to attend a university in

America. She has made the most of the opportunity, establishing a life there. She is now married and has started a family.

The following morning, I had another meeting with Bosco. He convinced me that there were additional students in the top two years of his primary school who would soon be in a similar position to that of Albert. If they were to continue with their education, they would need support at secondary school. He had singled out six students. He escorted me round the village to meet their families. Photographs were taken and each child was asked to produce a 'pro forma', giving a short synopsis of their family situation. As it happened, most of these turned out to be almost identical, being constructed in such a way as not to fail to tug at the heartstrings of anyone reading them. Although no promises were made, it seemed that my new charity might have to expand before it had been started. I could not support all six students, so other willing recruits would have to be found. Fortunately, the matter was not urgent, as the support was not required for at least another year. Being so conscious of the desperate need for help in so many different respects in this village, it was so difficult to be sensible about one's limitations and not to make promises that were unattainable. My initial desire was to help everyone, something that was just not possible when my resources were limited.

After lunch, Father Fabio introduced me to his group of fisherwomen, who were busy endeavouring to encircle a school of tilapia using a very large net. I was assured there were no crocodiles in the area, so there was no danger that either the women or the fish were likely to become the next meal for a hungry beast, but I did remain a little apprehensive watching them. The process was actually comical for both participant and spectator. There was no definitive attire for fishing, so the women waded into the lake with one hand gripping the net and the other endeavouring to hitch up their voluminous dresses. This apparel proved more of a hindrance than a help to any activity in the water. As the ability to swim was non-existent, the whole operation was extremely precarious. The idea was that the bravest, and often tallest, of the women would walk as far as possible into the lake, taking due diligence so as not to disappear into some unforeseen hole. Others would follow, gradually encircling a sizeable area of water, returning to the shore further along the lake. Eventually, women would be stationed at intervals along the net. Instructions would then be issued, asking them to commence walking towards the shore. The net had a series of weights to ensure that it dragged along the bottom of the lake. It was hoped that by the time the women reached the shore, any unfortunate fish would have become trapped. Needless to say, there was much stumbling, much chatting and much giggling! Fishing was a pastime to be enjoyed. By the time the women attained the safety of the shore, I was surprised that any fish had not managed to find a way to escape. Suffice it to say, the whole operation had bamboozled a few tilapia who had failed to extricate themselves from the confines of the net. These fish were unceremoniously despatched when they had been beached. Despite the obvious delight of the women at managing to catch anything, I was informed that it was not unknown to catch over fifty fish in such a manner. The fish would later be dried and salted. Trucking them south fetched reasonable profits for those involved in the endeavour.

My final task on this visit was to receive the artefacts that the women had made for me to sell in England. They had indeed been very busy, giving me a substantial portion of their wares. On this occasion, trust was not an issue. They understood that payment would not be forthcoming until I had actually sold the items. I was happy to be helping them, but I had failed to consider the sustainability of the project. At this stage, no thought had been given to the long-term future of what I was doing. Yes, undoubtedly there was a short-term gain, and for a few years the women earned a substantial income, but I could not sell their wares endlessly. Problems were to present themselves in the not-too-distant future.

The next day, I was woken by Father Andrew soon after 2.30 am in the morning as he wished to depart by 3 am. I was assured this was not related to the threat of bandits along the way (we would be taking a very different route to that of the outward journey); he simply wished to reach Nanyuki at the foot of Mount Kenya in good time, but needed to include a detour via Marsabit as teachers were attending a conference there. Instead of heading south, we set off in a northerly direction via North Horr, using the road I had apparently used for my very first visit on the notorious safari. At that time, this was actually the quickest direct route to Marsabit. Despite the inevitable puncture, we reached Marsabit at 9.30, in time for breakfast with another bishop. I was honoured, although I am certain that his presence at the meal was coincidental rather than planned for my benefit. I did seem to have a very fortunate knack of attracting prominent people to some of these meals.

The route south took us through Archers Post and Isiolo, stopping at one of the missionary outposts for a very welcome lunch. Yet again, progress was then impeded by the presence of the tarmac! I was fascinated by the fact that once again I was with a Kenyan driver who was happier on a dirt road. We arrived at our destination in the late afternoon. It was light enough to be able to enjoy a view of Mount Kenya; not that we could see more than the lower slopes, because it was enshrouded in cloud, apparently a very common occurrence. I had accumulated a substantial amount of dust about my person, especially in my hair, during my stay in Loiyangalani and as a result of the journey. It required a lengthy shower and washing of my hair to rid me of the various layers of dirt.

The journey to Nairobi was very straightforward but did include one interesting interlude. At one point, we were brought to a rather abrupt halt by a policeman standing in the middle of the road with an arm raised, which was initially rather alarming. Had he been notified of the contraband (the Kenyan artefacts) that I was about to smuggle out of the country? No, we were informed that the President of Kenya was about to pass through. Apparently, whenever the President travels by road, the route has to be cleared so that he and his considerable entourage can monopolise the road. I did note at the time that the escort seemed to be excessive; perhaps others had tagged along to enjoy a swift passage along what otherwise would have been a very congested road. Knowing the severity of the traffic jams in Nairobi, it came as no surprise that the President should take full advantage of this privilege. I am sure he was the only person who was assured of arriving on time for any appointment. I did consider that being caught up in traffic would not only delay the President but could make him the target for any potential assassin. Even though Kenya is comparatively safe, I am sure there are probably some who would be quite happy to initiate his demise, so the precautions were probably very wise.

Once in Nairobi, I did locate sufficient cash to purchase five large boxes of sanitary towels for Father Andrew to take back to Loiyangalani. As mentioned earlier, these were to be the first of many over the years. The sight of an Englishman struggling through the streets of Nairobi endeavouring to carry five very large boxes of sanitary towels may well have been a source of great amusement for fellow tourists. In all probability, I would most likely have collided with some unsuspecting fellow pedestrian, spilling the contents of the boxes across the pavement and possibly into the road. I was therefore most fortunate to procure the assistance of a couple of Kenyans who were only too happy to help.

Father Andrew and I were able to shepherd them across a couple of busy roads that needed to be crossed. Eventually, we reached the comparative safety of our vehicle. Our two 'porters' were very happy to have been able to help. I then repeated my efforts to persuade the cashiers at one of the banks to accept my traveller's cheques, as I had wanted to give Father Andrew some money. Inevitably, the attempt was in vain. I did manage to use my debit card yet again, but my bank balance was beginning to groan under the pressure to which it was being subjected. I had promised Bosco a phone that could be connected to the internet so that we could communicate by e-mail. Today this may seem a rather mundane request, but at that time phones with internet access were not a standard acquisition. Once procured, this did save us time and expense, as I had had to resort to expensive phone calls.

Father Andrew handed me over to Father Joya, who very kindly negotiated the traffic and deposited me at the airport later that evening for my journey home. Even in the late evening, the roads were heaving with various modes of transport, apparently so late in reaching their destinations that they demanded rite of passage over other more sedate users of the highway. The mode of driving is probably not unique to this country, but the way in which the Kenyans appeared to have grown accustomed to the situation surprised me. Granted, horns were used prolifically, but tempers seldom flared. There were some horrific accidents, but by and large travellers reached their destinations, possibly flustered but otherwise apparently unscathed. Many vehicles displayed battle scars of some description that revealed their encounters with other road users.

My journey to Kenya had ended amid many hopes and aspirations. I had much to contemplate and much to action upon my return to the UK.

CHAPTER SIX

Introduction to Friends

It was to be another three years before my next trip to Loiyangalani. Meanwhile, there had been developments.

Upon my return in 2009, I had been invited to speak at my local church about the trip and any future plans that I may have been considering. I was overwhelmed by the interest that was shown by the congregation. It was not long before I had sponsors for each of the six students who had been identified by Bosco as requiring assistance. Interest from others was so positive that I was able to establish a committee to oversee the activities of a new charity. The Loiyangalani Trust was founded later that year, soon becoming a registered charity. Within twelve months, matters had progressed further than I had ever dreamt as being possible. Money was flowing into the bank account and then being despatched to Loiyangalani on a regular basis. My desire to form a small charity to reclaim the gift aid on my donations for Albert's education had paled into insignificance. Bosco soon had money for a regular supply of sanitary towels, the construction of the extra desks and the purchase of food for his students. From acorns oak trees grow!

I was also able to extend my commitment to selling the artefacts for the women. I attended various events. As the items were cheap, had an appeal to youngsters and were funding a needy group of people, the public were very positive in their response. I had managed to procure further supplies utilising the kindness of one or two travellers returning from Kenya. Luckily, they had no qualms about being stopped and questioned as prospective smugglers of highly desirable contraband!

Communication with Bosco via his new phone using e-mails was working very well, so I could see no reason to return to Loiyangalani with affairs running so smoothly. Therefore, friends and members of the committee initiated the next visit. One evening, a group of us was attending a local barn dance, a fund-raising event organised by our church. I was asked by one of my friends when I would be returning to Loiyangalani for my next visit, because he would like to accompany me. The chair of the Loiyangalani Trust Committee also expressed an interest in visiting the village, as she wished to meet those with whom we were dealing. Soon, another lady had also declared that she too would like to accompany us. Arrangements were made and we decided upon a visit in February 2012. I realised that asking my companions to undergo the uncertainties associated with the journey by road from Nairobi was not a good idea. It was important for the adventure to be as enjoyable as possible. We decided that a compromise was necessary, so we opted for a flight to Marsabit, travelling onwards by road from there.

We were met by Father Joya at Nairobi Airport. By this time, he had been promoted within the Consolata hierarchy and was now the head of the Consolata mission in Kenya. Given that he was the first non-Italian to hold this position, it was a sign of the considerable respect and high regard with which his superiors in Italy and fellow priests in Kenya viewed him. Judging by the subsequent increase in the circumference of his waistline, I imagine that his new role necessitated a rather sedentary lifestyle! To find the time to meet and assist us upon our arrival was extremely kind.

The journey to the Consolata mission in Langata was a very swift and rather frustrating introduction for my travelling companions to the joys (and hazards) of road transport in Nairobi. It took longer than it should have done to make the comparatively short journey from the airport, with Father Joya commenting that he was certain the situation had improved since my last visit. Apparently, traffic regulations had been introduced, particularly to curb some of the more alarming activities of the infamous *matatus*. I confess that I failed to notice any significant difference!

After settling into our allocated accommodation, we wandered across to the Westlands shopping centre with the specific aim of obtaining a preferable rate to exchange our money into Kenyan shillings. No traveller's cheques this time! Like many transactions in Kenya, there is always the opportunity to barter. This necessitated visiting more than one bank, but did ensure that we received the most favourable exchange rate for our money. Upon returning to the mission, I had to await the arrival of Bibles from the Kenya Bible Society. The congregation from my church had very kindly provided money to purchase Bibles for the students at the primary school. Although we could have carried Bibles with us, purchasing Bibles in England that were in Swahili would probably have been beyond the scope of most Christian bookshops!

The following day, Father Joya kindly drove us to Wilson Airport, a smaller airport that caters for internal flights. We had booked a flight with Mission Aviation Fellowship (MAF). They cover most areas in Kenya, but being a voluntary organisation, they do not offer flights to tourists other than in exceptional circumstances. Being volunteers for a registered charity and armed with a copious supply of Bibles, we apparently qualified! They were suitably impressed to permit us to travel on one of their planes. Once accepted as *bona fide*, we had no problems using them on further visits. As the plane was not the largest in which I had flown, weight was crucial, which was where the Bibles proved a slight disadvantage. On their own, they probably accounted for our total baggage allowance, so unless we were to do without our personal baggage, each of us had to be weighed! This was a very public affair, with no opportunity for any data protection or privacy surrounding the actual weights. Luckily, my three companions could not be described as overweight, and so after hasty calculations, it was decided that the plane would manage to take off with the four of us, Bibles and baggage! There was no need for any hasty repacking! Father Joya must have been quite relieved that he did not have to nurse a variety of discarded items on his return journey to the mission!

The aircraft seated ten, so we were not alone. I think we were all relieved when the wheels finally left the runway and the plane commenced its ascent. We flew close to Mount Kenya, which was a treat. At least I was able to observe the upper section of the mountain, which had remained so obstinately hidden behind cloud upon my previous visit. The pilot kept us informed as to the various landmarks as they appeared below the aircraft. It was very interesting to observe the country from the air. As Marsabit is some distance due east of Lake Turkana, there was no opportunity to enjoy views of the lake.

Arriving in Marsabit, we were met by Bosco, a driver and two companions, who were to accompany us to Loiyangalani. We were escorted to a local café to partake of lunch. I remarked in my diary that the meal was "interesting" which probably means that I had not the remotest idea what I was eating and probably no wish to do so. Having become wary as to the nature of any meat that was likely to be on offer,

I tended to be choosy where possible. We then wandered through the shopping area purchasing a few items, mainly fruit, to accompany us to Loiyangalani. No apples this time! I was a little surprised that there appeared to be little urgency to depart; perhaps I should not have been as we were in Kenya! We finally left Marsabit at 2.30 pm. Having some idea as to the length of the journey ahead, I realised that it would be dark when we reached Loiyangalani. I discovered that a detour via South Horr had been planned. Although South Horr is on the direct route from Maralal, it involves a diversion when travelling from Marsabit of about an hour each way. It would be dark long before reaching Loiyangalani!

The journey to South Horr was uneventful. Upon arrival, we were served supper at the mission. This was the last time that I was to meet Father Gallino, the priest who had been in residence in Loiyangalani when I commenced my sponsorship of the two boys. He was to die shortly after our visit. After supper we visited Nyeri Boys' Secondary School, where two of the boys being sponsored via the charity were pupils. As the visit was nocturnal, we could not enter the school grounds, so various messages had to be conveyed via the night watchman to the two boys to enable them to meet us and collect a few 'goodies' that had been allocated to them, mainly pencils and other items of stationery. Fortunately, they had not yet retired for the night.

With at least four hours of travelling remaining, I alone of the visiting party realised just how late our arrival at our destination would be. It had been a long day, so this final section was undertaken with very little chatter. Fatigue had set in, but during the four-hour journey, travelling conditions were not conducive to any form of sleep. There was one memorable event approximately halfway to Loiyangalani. The driver had to stop the vehicle because, he told us, he needed to "kill a snake". Although this was not to be taken literally, what he actually did would certainly have distressed any snake! We managed to have a short break and so extricated ourselves from the vehicle. With a total absence of light (the driver had kindly doused the vehicle lights), the panorama overhead was a sight never to be forgotten. The clarity was such that one felt one could reach out and touch the stars. Being relatively close to the equator, it was an opportunity for us to observe the night sky with both The Southern Cross and The Plough being visible at opposite ends of the vista.

We also managed to spot an aardvark, which evaded us successfully, unlike the poor ostriches on my previous trip. Apparently, they are only seen at night. We arrived at our destination, the Palm Shade (safari)

Camp, at 2.30 in the morning. Although Benedict had long since retired to bed, some poor soul had been designated to await our arrival and escort us to our huts. We were given much needed refreshments before retiring. Each of us had our own hut, which contained little more than a bed, a small table and chair, and an en suite facility consisting of toilet, shower and basin. As with all our showers in Loiyangalani, the temperature of the water was fixed, no hot or cold taps; an arrangement that certainly reduces any plumbing costs!

Benedict was on hand to greet us at breakfast. He had not been surprised by the lateness of our arrival. We were in no hurry to participate in anything other than breakfast, so it was a leisurely affair. The communal dining area was situated in a location very central to the camp, so was a gathering place for anyone visiting. We were to use it frequently for meetings with various people. Bosco escorted us on a guided tour of the town. Laura's house was on the list of locations to be visited. Again, she was very pleased to see me. We did not stay long as she was not well; providing hospitality for the four of us and Bosco would have been too much to ask.

We then headed to the primary school and discovered how easy it is in Loiyangalani to move from comparative obscurity to a status of stardom in seconds! Soon after the charity had been established, we had decided to produce leaflets to publicise our endeavours. I was fortunate to find a talented young lady in the UK to make the most of the photographs that I had taken on my previous visit. For the front cover, she had used part of a very innocuous photo that I had taken of some of the children as they were milling around in the school grounds at lunchtime. The section she used focuses on a young girl carrying a dish walking towards me. We had copies of the leaflet with us and showed them to staff and pupils alike. As soon as the 'star' of the leaflet had been identified, a search was mounted to locate her. The poor girl had no idea as to the reason behind her sudden promotion to stardom until she was shown the leaflet. She was, of course, three years older and obviously susceptible to shyness, so the whole experience was traumatic, to say the least. The photo had been taken in such a way that she would have no recollection of being in the picture. As the leaflet was viewed by more people, her status continued to rise in the community, and she was compelled to accommodate this short-term elevation of status to that of a celebrity. Children in other pictures in the leaflet also received acclaim but not quite at the level of this young lady.

We gave Bosco the 'goodies# that had accompanied us from England. He distributed those and the Bibles after our departure, as they were to be used as rewards for attainment. We had also brought some tennis balls, being the only type of ball produced in England that stood any chance of surviving the thorns and rocky terrain. Bosco did show us the desks that had been constructed from money we had sent previously. He had written the name of our village on some of them as being an indication as from where the money had originated. Being a small village, I am sure no other visitor would have been able to locate it on any map of England, but the gesture was greatly appreciated. Others had been inscribed "donated by the Loiyangalani Trust". As far as I know, some of these desks are still in use.

After lunch, we visited Father Andrew in the mission. The swimming pool was an obvious attraction, and we were invited to use it as and when we wished. We then went for our walkabout in the village area in the southern section of the complex. The four of us attracted much attention wherever we roamed. The occupants of huts that we visited were always delighted to see us and grateful for what we were doing. My companions were as amazed as I had been by the apparent joy exhibited, particularly by the children. It was to have a lasting impression on them. There was no shortage of young children trying to grasp one of the eight available hands! Again, I witnessed the magnificent sunset as the sun disappeared behind the lake. It is a sight that is destined to remain with the beholder for ever. Supper and refreshments were most welcome back at our base after our wander.

The accommodation at Palm Shade Camp was certainly preferable to that in the mission. Undesirables such as scorpions and snakes were kept well away. Mosquito nets were provided, although not necessary. Mosquitos were present in the swampy areas of the village, but not so in most other places. As there is an incessant gale blowing during the day, it is sufficient to keep most insects at bay. The wind drops at night, but more often than not, there is still a light breeze. The trick is to be able to direct any breeze that may be present at night to assist with one's capacity to be able to snatch some sleep. I was not averse to taking a shower in the middle of the night as a way of reducing my body temperature.

The following day, we returned to the primary school for a more formal visit. The students entertained us with a wonderful display of singing and dancing. Africans have an innate ability to move to the rhythms of dance. Watching them, one senses that they enjoy expressing themselves through this medium. They also develop the ability to sing in tune at a young age. The combination of both talents was very much in evidence during this display. They had composed lyrics in English that expressed their thanks for what we were doing. This was greatly appreciated. It was also an opportunity to exchange their school uniforms for tribal attire, which gave the display an extra dimension. After the performance, we were taken to each of the classrooms to meet the students. Away from singing and dancing, the individuals are extremely shy, so trying to engage in conversation with pupils, especially in the lower classes, was a challenge.

We were asked to sign our names in the visitors' book. I was amused to see that upon my visit in 2005, mine had been the first name in the book. At least that was proof to my colleagues that stories of my previous visits to Loiyangalani had not been completely fabricated!

The next task was to participate in a tree-planting ceremony to mark our visit. I thought such events were usually the demesne of royal visitors. As royalty of any description were unlikely to honour Loiyangalani with their presence, we were unworthy substitutes. Upon a subsequent visit, I discovered that unfortunately my tree was one of three of the four that had withered and died. Green fingers I certainly have not. We visited the school workshop, where more desks were being constructed. It was good to see that local labour was used in the construction, once the materials had been procured from elsewhere.

We walked over to the secondary school. I was very disappointed to discover that the science block remained incomplete. The roof appeared to have been abandoned partway through construction, so the contents of the building were covered in a layer of dust. In another room, boxes of computer equipment remained unopened. These were destined to be used in the science building. It was a reminder as to how easy it is to 'put the cart before the horse'. The equipment had been ordered and supplied without first ensuring that the building in which it was to be used had been completed. Because the school was short of students, the number of teachers had been reduced. As a result, teachers had to teach subjects for which they were not properly qualified. Some subjects were not offered; for example, there was a vacancy for a physics teacher. My student, Albert, was there to greet me. He was unhappy about the facilities, telling me that at night he was compelled to study by candlelight. The fact that he later achieved a 'B' grade in his studies, while the remainder of his fellow students failed to achieve anything higher than a 'D', says a great deal about his motivation, determination and ability. The four of us visiting would have liked to have been able to offer financial assistance to the school, but with our commitments to the primary school and students at other secondary schools, we would have rapidly become overstretched.

We then visited the women's group. We had more money to give them from the sales of their artefacts in England, so they continued to be most appreciative of all that I was doing for them. Needless to say, we would be given yet more items to take back to England with us, the quantity of which was to raise the first questions regarding the legality of what we were being asked to do.[13]

During our visit there was a 'Peace Camp' for children from Year Six being coordinated for the benefit of pupils from each of the primary schools in the local area. It should be noted that 'local' does not have quite the same connotations as it might do in most countries. Some of these students belonged to primary schools that were fifty or more miles away. The camp had been organised for the duration of a week with the sole aim of bringing together children from the different tribes. Historically, there has always been intertribal conflict, usually in the form of the raiding of herds of livestock from neighbouring tribes. Often these raids resulted not only in the abduction of livestock, but also physical conflict that could involve the loss of life. Although less frequent now, raiding still occurred, especially in times of drought when herds had been devastated. It was, though, vital for the future of the country that the strength of tribal affiliations be modified so that those from different tribes could exist alongside each other cooperating for the common good. Concepts such as Peace Camps were extremely important for nurturing this idea at a young age. We were permitted to observe some of the activities during our visit, giving encouragement where appropriate.

The following day, we were driven to the El Molo village. The highlight of this visit was to be a boat trip that very nearly failed to materialise. The boat that had been allocated for the trip stubbornly refused to go anywhere, much to the dismay of the owner. As I previously noted, Kenyans generally solve most problems of a mechanical nature, but for whatever reason, this problem seemed to be unsolvable! Help was at hand. An alternative means of transport was found. It appeared that

---

[13] See page 97 for more discussion on this.

another boat owner possessed a boat that was decidedly more cooperative. We duly embarked and set off on our excursion.

It was pointless to enquire about the presence of anything that might be termed as safety equipment (for example, life jackets), although things were to change. It did cross my mind that if the engine on this boat decided that it wished to function no more, we could be in a very interesting situation. It was one thing breaking down in a vehicle on dry land, but being stranded on the lake could pose an array of possibilities. Coastguards and other such forms of rescue did not exist, and the idea of swimming in what were crocodile-infested waters was not appealing. I imagine that as we were not that far from shore, we would have had to resort to frantic waving and gesticulating in the hope that yet another craft could be mustered to come to our rescue. Boats do venture out some distance, but many are powered by sails, which are fabricated by stitching together old sacks, ingenious but probably not that reliable in strong winds. Suffice it to say that these vessels have come to grief, usually resulting in the loss of life of the entire crew. Swimming is almost totally unknown amongst the locals. The brother of Raphael, a student I was to sponsor in the coming years, was lost in this manner. Fish tend to be larger and more plentiful further from the shore, so the desire to brave the unpredictable conditions on the lake tends to persist. Fortunately, we were only visiting an island that necessitated a very short journey. It was on a future trip that I was to experience the true character of the lake! Our trip proceeded without any cause for alarm, so we were able to disembark safely once we had returned to shore.

After lunch, we again returned to the primary school. Potential sponsors enjoy photographs of their students, so those pupils who had been singled out as potential candidates for sponsorship were lined up against the school wall individually so that they could be photographed. Some of these photos were little more than 'mug shots' which did not flatter the students. As with my previous visit, they were asked to produce 'pro formas' describing their family and their circumstances. Yet again, there was a common thread that seemed to be present in each of them. There was little variety in the content, but the sponsors would only see the one relating to their particular student, so there was no cause for concern. Although nothing was promised to the individual students, because at that stage we would have to find additional sponsors, we did manage to honour our commitment to each of them. We have continued to be very lucky in that we have as yet never failed to find a sponsor for a student when it has been needed. We do limit our commitment for that very reason.

The following morning, I again attended the Peace Camp while my fellow travellers were making use of the swimming pool. I had mentioned to the organisers that I had been involved with youth groups in the past and could introduce them to one of the games from my repertoire. This seemed as good a time as any. I had brought a whistle with me because I had had in mind what I thought to be a relatively simple game that would involve participation by all the children and, so I rather erroneously believed, would be relatively easy to explain despite possible language difficulties.

The game exists under a variety of names, one of which is 'cat and mouse'. The children stand in rows, at approximately arm's length from their neighbours, left, right, front and behind. Initially, all face in the same direction with their arms extended. The situation resembles a rectangular grid with a child at each point on the grid. Two children are selected to be 'cat' and 'mouse' respectively. The 'cat' then chases the 'mouse' along the rows created by the children standing in the grid. When the 'cat' appears to be closing in on the 'mouse', the whistle is blown, so that all the students execute a quarter turn, thereby ensuring that the original rows are blocked so that the pursuit of 'cat' and 'mouse' resumes in a direction at ninety degrees to the original direction. The whistle can then be blown at any time so that the direction of the pursuit is changed either to favour the 'cat' or the 'mouse', each time necessitating a quarter turn.

It all sounds very straightforward. I had to explain the rules to one of the leaders who then translated them into Swahili. Whether anything was lost in translation, I do not know. Things started well, but as soon as the whistle was blown, chaos! Some students rotated correctly, some incorrectly and some not at all. Arms appeared to be extended in all directions, with pupils resembling malfunctioning windmills! Further instructions were issued. When the whistle was blown again, a larger proportion of the students seem to have understood what was expected. Where mistakes were made, neighbours generally managed to convey useful information to ensure that eventually the blowing of the whistle had the desired effect and the arms rotated in the correct direction in unison. It was interesting to observe the behaviour of the 'cat' and the 'mouse'; both were liable to attempt to break through barriers in exactly the same way as youngsters had done in England when playing the game.

The desire to bend the rules seems to exist wherever the game is played. Once the game was flowing, there was a great deal of hilarity, screaming and shouting, so the children appeared to enjoy themselves. Whether the leaders were ever to use the game again, I have no idea.

Arrangements were made with Father Andrew to borrow the mission vehicle with a driver to take us to Gatab, the village in Mount Kulal. It had been decided we should also take a mechanic. Perhaps the driver had little mechanical knowledge. As Bosco had also decided to accompany us, the net result of this decision was that I was one of four men crammed into the rear of a vehicle that was designed to seat no more than three, reminiscent of a previous journey that I had undertaken in similar conditions. Fortunately, the other three required less space than me! I did comment in my diary that the back seat could have benefitted from extra padding. I have previously described the hazards of this trip when first visiting this village with Father Joya. It appeared that time was of little importance, and so we were able to stop at our leisure to photograph the views when ascending the mountain, something I had not been able to do on my previous visit. The view across the arid area to Lake Turkana is majestic. We were able to spot Loiyangalani, but without binoculars the identification of individual buildings was not possible. Picnic lunch had been provided by Benedict and was consumed upon reaching the village. Sitting down to consume the food ensured that we attracted the attention of the local children. Initially, we were approached with a degree of shyness, but once they discovered we were not ogres from some foreign planet, their expressions changed. We were then treated to radiant smiles. We were very much a curiosity. I am certain tourists do visit the village, but probably more infrequently than they do Loiyangalani.

On the return journey, we spent time looking down into the spectacular gorge. Apparently, it is possible to walk through this gorge, but at times the path is very narrow with high cliffs on either side. It is not a venture to be undertaken without considerable preparation; most definitely out of our league on this occasion! Unlike my previous trip, we were not flagged down by locals along the way. Whether water was less scarce or whether the nomads were elsewhere, I never did discover. I was more concerned about the lack of comfort in the rear of the vehicle and the consequent turbulence that I was experiencing during the journey. Needless to say, arriving in Loiyangalani was a delightful relief.

The various schools attending the Peace Camp had each been asked to prepare an item involving singing and dancing. We were invited to attend the performance. The individual nature of each act was very much in evidence. Whether this was due to subtle differences regarding the location of each school, I have no idea. These acts were most entertaining and delivered with obvious enthusiasm and enjoyment. As children may spend several years in a single year group, each performance contained children of varying ages, which enhanced the displays.

We returned to Palm Shade Camp for supper. This was always a time to reflect on the activities of the day. We were often joined by others from the village. Bosco was a permanent fixture at these meals. He seemed to enjoy eating with us. This was not solely a reflection of his hospitable nature. As Benedict's cooks surpassed themselves, there was also a fair chance that home cooking was unable to match delights of that produced at Palm Shade Camp.

The following day was Sunday and our final day in Loiyangalani. The morning was spent attending Mass. We were each invited to say a few words at the end of the service, the bulk of which was translated, although the knowledge of English is moderately widespread. Applause and laughter seemed to be spontaneous in most of the expected places without the need for the interpreter. Unfortunately, we were being assigned celebrity status. This is inevitable when one has the means to assist a community experiencing various degrees of poverty. It is certainly not something that we sought and remains something that I would like to have avoided. We had expressed an interest in helping the community financially, and indeed, they had experienced the fruits of our assistance. Achieving a status amongst a group of people that one could never experience in one's own country can lead to inflated ideas of self-importance and excesses that may accompany such feelings. To me, it was important to exercise humility without taking advantage of any potentially damaging inflation of one's status or ego. We are human beings in the same way as those in the village. We simply have the lucky advantage of possessing significant wealth to assist those who do not have such resources.

After lunch, we were involved in a meeting with Bosco and several prominent members of the community. We had decided that decisions should not rest with Bosco. By seeking advice from a committee, this would ensure that he could not be accused of making decisions that would favour one particular family or, more importantly, one particular tribe. I was pleased to discover that Benedict had decided that he would join the committee. We discussed ways in which funding should be allocated. The committee would produce a list of requests in order of priority. We would then decide which of these the Trust had the resources to fund at any given time. Regarding the children to be sponsored, the fact that the committee members represented the three main tribes would ensure that the selection criteria would not favour one tribe. It was critical that the selection process would be such that its outcome could be justified to any individual questioning the decisions. We also suggested that an accounting procedure be used whereby all transactions, both income and expenditure, could be noted so that there was total transparency. This meeting proved to be extremely worthwhile and laid the foundations for procedures that were to assist greatly in the allocation of funds over the forthcoming years.

We then visited the women with the beaded artefacts. As mentioned earlier, significant quantities of items had been produced. Although this did not bother me, my travelling companions were concerned. It was not the additional weight for their baggage allowance (we were travelling very light anyway); it was the transit through customs that concerned them. We were not seeking to make money for ourselves from these items. As all proceeds from the sales were being despatched directly to the women in Loiyangalani, in all honesty we had nothing to declare. However, if we were to be stopped in customs and our 'loot' was discovered, what would we say? Beaded items could hardly be termed as contraband, but they did have a value. If we could not prove that the money from the sales was indeed being returned to those who had made the items, were we actually smuggling? Being arrested and categorised in the same group as those involved in the smuggling of genuine contraband was not something that appealed. On this occasion, my companions decided to comply with my wishes on the understanding that this would be the only time that they should be involved in this procedure. As it happened, we were not to be stopped, but the realisation that perhaps we were 'sailing close to the wind' was probably the beginning of the end of this venture. I was compelled to consider very carefully the exact nature and consequences of what I was doing.

We were treated to another memorable supper by Benedict's staff. We shared the feast with as many friends as was feasible to ensure that we could thank those who had been so cooperative and hospitable during our visit.

Benedict's camp does attract some very adventurous types. The following morning, as we were having breakfast, a French family arrived with five children. They had driven from South Africa and were heading north through Ethiopia and other countries on their expedition back to France. They were well prepared for the journey, but Ethiopia is not the safest country through which to drive. I hope that they eventually reached their destination without any nasty experiences.

Soon after breakfast, we said our farewells and made preparations for our departure. There were no detours planned on this occasion. We were to head directly to Marsabit without visiting South Horr. As is customary, there were extra passengers. Unlike my previous journey with Father Andrew, we used the southern route, as one of the passengers wished to disembark en route. In my diary, I described the journey as being "fast" and "extremely uncomfortable". There is also reference to a "numb bum". Perhaps one day I will discover a vehicle that has sufficient space and padding to allow me to travel in this country with a modicum of comfort!

We stopped in a small village called Kargi.[14] Lunch consisted of pancakes. We then proceeded to Marsabit, where we were staying overnight at a hostel as our flight south was scheduled for the following day. Supper was provided before Bosco escorted us to a bar in town to enjoy the 'nightlife' of Marsabit. The refreshments were much appreciated but there was little in the way of entertainment! Perhaps it would have been more than inappropriate for four middle-aged visitors from England to endeavour to 'paint the town red'!

Accommodation was spartan but adequate. We were asked to be economical with the water when having showers as there was a shortage in the town. Although it would have been very pleasant to linger in the shower for some time after the dusty journey, I decided that I did not wish to be responsible for ensuring the water situation deteriorated any further due to my excesses, so I complied with the request.

The next day, after breakfast, we experienced some shopping – only with our eyes, as our financial resources were inadequate for significant purchases. We then returned to the hostel to discover that news had filtered through that the flight had been severely delayed. No specific reason was given, but hopefully it had been nothing mechanical! We spent the early part of the afternoon kicking our heels in downtown Marsabit, which was a little taxing as we had accomplished all that we wished to accomplish and the attractions were quite limited. Lunch was

[14] See page 111 for another adventure involving Kargi.

taken at the same premises we had used on the outward journey. At least we knew what to expect, even if we were not entirely certain as to what we were eating. I believe one or two of my companions were a little more choosey over what they selected from the menu than they had been last time!

Eventually, news filtered through that the plane was about to arrive, so we were driven to the airstrip. Despite the extra cargo of bracelets, weighing and measuring was unnecessary on this occasion, as the plane was far from full. We said our farewells to Bosco and embarked on our journey south. The flight passed on the other side of Mount Kenya so that we were given the opportunity to view it from a different perspective. The ever-dependable Father Joya was at Wilson Airport to meet us. His day had been impeded by the delay to the flight, but as ever, he seemed unruffled. Despite his heavy workload, he continued to ensure that we were well looked after.

The following day was spent visiting various Consolata establishments, one of which is a technical college. We were to use this on several occasions for students who needed technical education. That evening, three of us were taken to the main airport for our return journey, as one member of our group had decided to extend the visit to include a safari trip.

It is amazing how visits of this nature affect people. The chair of our committee admitted that for her the visit was life-changing. Although she was to visit Loiyangalani again on future occasions, this was the visit that was to ensure her lifelong involvement with the charity. There is no doubt that Loiyangalani has a special attraction. To me, it is the fact that its inhabitants are content with so little and yet they are so grateful for the little they do have. They live uncomplicated lives, but they are accustomed to hardship with which they deal as best they can. Despite the obvious suffering, they have learnt to smile. They have also learnt genuinely to appreciate the help that they are offered by anyone who is interested in them. We have much to learn from these people in our so-called 'affluent society'. The radiance with which the faces of the young children light up should be beacons of sunshine to us.

CHAPTER SEVEN

The Incredible Journey

My next visit to Loiyangalani was in February 2013. Having not found any need to visit Loiyangalani on a regular basis, it may seem strange that I had decided to return only a year after my previous visit. The company for which I was working at the time decided to support me in my endeavours, initially by volunteering to pay for a flight to Loiyangalani each year. Unfortunately, as with many things that appear to be too good to be true, the situation changed, and the offer was subsequently downgraded to facilitate the sponsorship of students instead. Realistically, assisting students was a preferable means of utilising the firm's generosity. Travelling to Loiyangalani each year was unnecessary, given the rapid improvement in communications, unless there was a major problem. Costly long-distance phone calls had been replaced by wonders such as e-mails. Nevertheless, on this occasion, the offer of financial assistance for a flight had been made, and so I decided to accept it graciously. As it happened, this was to be the worst-planned of my trips, resulting in an 'epic' journey.

The omens were not good from the moment I landed in Nairobi. Due to a misunderstanding, the ever-reliable Father Joya was nowhere to be seen. I was faced with two immediate dilemmas. Not only did I not recall the address of the Consolata mission in Nairobi, but I also possessed no Kenyan shillings with which to pay any taxi driver. I had little cash on me as I had planned to withdraw cash from my account using one of the banks in Nairobi to purchase the Kenyan shillings. I had also been warned that changing money at the airport was inadvisable as the exchange rate did not favour tourists. Fortunately, I discovered a taxi driver who not only seemed to know the location of the mission, but who was also convinced that the fare would be forthcoming from someone at the mission who would kindly loan me what I required upon my arrival. Would a Kenyan tourist in a similar predicament arriving at Heathrow Airport have received similar treatment? It is unnecessary to comment upon the scenario that would have unfolded! I believe the fact that I was being hosted by the mission rather than frequenting one of the more expensive hotels in Nairobi probably assisted in convincing the driver that my intentions were genuine and that he would not be out of pocket. He also offered me what turned out to be a favourable rate for the journey. Arriving at the mission, he was duly paid, and I was able to instigate the necessary reimbursement after visiting one of the banks. Father Joya was very apologetic about his non-attendance at the airport.

My departure for Loiyangalani had been arranged for 10 am the following morning. Father Andrew was to be my driver. As it happened, I was still very much attached to my seat in the lobby of the building at lunchtime. I was therefore able to partake of a light lunch. Little did I know at the time that this was to be my final meal before breakfast the following morning! Father Andrew had obviously decided that feeding me on the journey was not of paramount importance. Perhaps I gave the impression that I was not in urgent need of sustenance! It was 1.45 pm when I finally boarded the vehicle, and we commenced our journey north. At this stage, so I noted in my diary, we had additional passengers but also breathing space!

We reached Nanyuki where, for some reason, the vehicle was unloaded and repacked. Not wanting to ask too many questions, I simply accepted that there must have been a logical explanation. I was handed a bottle of water, for which I was most grateful. We resumed our journey, stopping next at Isiolo where, to my astonishment, we were required to accommodate Benedict and another six passengers. There were four of us compressed on to the back seat, which normally seats two or three uncomfortably. Five additional poor souls were allocated 'luggage' accommodation, being asked to find spaces amongst the cargo in the very rear of the vehicle. Whether the vehicle was licensed to carry this number of passengers, I very much doubt! Any thought of being able to execute a hasty exit in the case of an emergency was swiftly dispelled!

Unbeknown to me, Father Andrew's plan was to drive through the night. He seemed to enjoy driving at night. In many countries, one could encounter any number of night-time wanderers from the animal kingdom, but he was convinced that such encounters were unlikely on this journey. It was certainly cooler, but what little view there was to enjoy from the relative discomfort of the journey was enshrouded in total darkness. There was a co-driver who shared the driving, but Father Andrew was obviously happier behind the wheel than as a passenger, so he did the lion's share of the driving. It was only when we reached the escarpment that I had any idea as to where we were. The fact that the four of us were wedged together like sardines in a tin shielded us from the worst of the rough and tumble. How those ensconced amongst the luggage managed to remain in their locations without somehow being propelled forward to join us in our seats, I have no idea. They had little or nothing with which to brace themselves.

We arrived in Loiyangalani soon after 7.15 in the morning. I again stayed at Palm Shade Camp. I was able to have a shower and breakfast. I am not sure which of the two was more welcome, given the nature of my journey. I then retired to bed for some much-needed sleep. I had now travelled just about every possible road to Loiyangalani and suffered just about every possible discomfort. I was confident that any future journey would be less of an ordeal. How wrong I was!

I am uncertain as to whether Bosco had been aware as to the nature of my journey to Loiyangalani. I had only been asleep for a matter of minutes before there was a knock on the door to my hut, which roused me from my slumber. I was pleased to see Bosco, but I would have been grateful if he could have waited a little longer before greeting me. He had planned a meeting with the students that we were sponsoring and so my presence was required in the dining area. We chatted about the progress made by the students in their studies. Some had performed better than others, so there was the inevitable spiel from me asking them to make the most of their opportunity. Naturally, I was assured that grades would improve forthwith. The students were very appreciative of the sponsorship that they were receiving. During my visit, gifts were produced for me to hand over to their sponsors upon my return to England. The care with which gifts are made never ceases to amaze me. I have one particular belt, given to me by Bosco, which must have involved hours of patient stitching. It is always very moving to receive a gift from someone who has fabricated it themselves rather than purchasing it.

Bosco escorted me to the primary school, where I was introduced to the students being considered for future sponsorship. Again, photos were taken and 'pro formas' written for me to convey to potential sponsors upon my return to England. I chatted to them, again stressing the importance of making the most of their opportunities.

As I had had relative success with the game 'cat and mouse' on my previous visit, I asked Bosco if I could introduce the children to other games from my repertoire. He was very happy for me to do so.

I was about to discover yet again the potential hazards and pitfalls in games that normally require very little in the way of explanation. The first game required the students to be numbered, standing in two rows opposite each other. It soon became apparent that a game that requires numbering in a foreign language and quick reactions from those allocated that particular number is immediately doomed to failure, particularly if the organiser speaks in a manner not familiar to the children. Although the children understood English, they were accustomed to hearing it spoken by their teachers. My middle-class accent was something very different. As it is, we often find it problematic to distinguish numbers such as five and nine; the problem was obviously compounded for these children. Perhaps a comparable situation could be imagined if English children were involved in a game played in Germany with a German teacher calling out numbers such as Ein, Zwei and Drei, all of which can be confused by an untrained ear. After very limited success with this game, I decided to teach them a game that required fairly basic instructions.

The game in question proved to be very popular, entailing much hilarity, screaming and general enjoyment despite a few bumps and scrapes along the way! The game was known to me as 'jockeys and horses'. The children were paired off, forming two circles, one member of the pair being in the outer circle and one in the inner. Each child in the inner circle was the 'horse' and had very little to do. The child in the outer circle was the 'jockey' and enjoyed most of the action. Upon the command of "Go!", the 'jockey' has to crawl through the legs of the 'horse' and then run round the 'horse' completing one and a half revolutions in a clockwise direction, a point that was actually open to abuse. Upon completing these revolutions, the 'jockey' then runs round the complete outer circle in a clockwise direction. Upon returning to the 'horse', the 'jockey' then leaps on to the 'horse' and is held in a piggyback position. The last pair completing the task is eliminated. Sometimes this may be a very wobbly pair that ends up collapsing, a 'faller'! The exercise is repeated continuously so that the number of pairs gradually diminishes until there is an outright winning pair. Not too complicated, or so I thought! What could possibly go wrong?

As it happened, just about everything, although no serious misadventures. Initially, the scene was fairly chaotic, with children running in all directions; often those endeavouring to run in the wrong direction were flattened by those proceeding in the correct direction. Once order had been established and the participants understood in which direction they should run in order to avoid being trampled upon, it was interesting that pairs attempted the shortcut identical to that used by their counterparts when playing the game in England. The one and a half revolutions round the 'horse' were curtailed to become half a revolution! Observant supervisors had to be alerted to this, with culprits either being disqualified or advised that they needed to amend their actions. The game was not reserved for boys only, with a fair number of girls willing to participate. However, the girls had an unforeseen disadvantage. Their uniforms, which consisted of long dresses, were a distinct handicap, not being designed for speedy progress running round a circle. Also, trying to attain the position of 'jockey' on the 'horse' at the end of each sequence was fraught with difficulty, involving desperate attempts to hitch up the skirts at the last minute while endeavouring to maintain a respectable degree of modesty. It was, therefore, the younger boys who seemed to excel.

One major difference between the game as played in England was the distribution of the roles. Pairs in England generally organised themselves so that the speedier individual played the role of 'jockey' and the more substantial one the role of 'horse'. On this occasion in Kenya, the participants were generally of similar size and exchanged roles for each repetition of the exercise. It was good to see the concept of sharing being promoted amongst the participants. Although there was a similar desire to win, it seemed important to each pair to create a genuine partnership ensuring the sharing of the roles. It also appeared to be played in great spirit with many smiles and few grumbles, even when pairs were eliminated. There was also greater audience participation with the ever-increasing crowd of spectators as pairs were eliminated. Often, the spectators seemed to enjoy the game as much as those participating. Needless to say, this game was a great success, and it was organised more than once during this visit.

I did attempt to play another game which is often referred to as 'helicopter', but it required my participation and I had neglected to take into account the severity of the heat. This game is very simple. The children stand in a circle and I stand in the middle with a shoe tied to the end of a rope. I then rotate the shoe at varying speeds and heights round the circle. The children jump as the shoe passes under them. The trick is to time the jump so that one clears the shoe without landing on it. In the confines of a cool hall in England, it is quite easy to ensure the shoe travels in such a way that height and speed can be varied catching out unwary individuals. Outside in the heat of Kenya, it was a disaster waiting to happen. I failed to catch many unwary participants before I collapsed in a dizzy heap, having to be rescued and removed to the comparative safety of one of the classrooms where I could recover after receiving copious amounts of water. This was the one and only time that I attempted this game! The staff were very kind, but I am certain one or two had a discrete chuckle at this mad Englishman attempting such a ridiculous game under these conditions! They were always so appreciative of any well-intended initiative, so I hoped they could forgive a few disasters along the way. I decided that I should supervise rather than participate in any games whilst in Loiyangalani.

I was also made very welcome by the ladies. They had greatly appreciated the significant sums of money that I had been able to make on their behalf. They were very careful with the proceeds from the sales. Obviously, much of the money received was distributed amongst themselves and part was used to purchase new materials. They also put aside a substantial amount in order to build themselves a compound. This involved the erection of two or three huts with a goat-proof stockade built round the perimeter. The huts were used for paid accommodation. They grew their own produce within the compound. The stockade walls ensured that their plants did not become a snack for any hungry goats who happened to be wandering in the vicinity. I was impressed with the enterprise, as it too would become a source of income for them. I was given another vast quantity of goods to take back to England with me. This was to be the last consignment, as it was becoming apparent that the project was becoming unsustainable, reliant upon a very dubious method of transportation between the two countries.

I had what was to be my last meeting with Laura. Magdalene had completed her studies and had married a doctor. The pair now worked in one of the dispensaries. Magdalene was most grateful to be employed in a way that not only meant she was able to help her community but also ensured that she was earning money that would be used to support the children that she was to produce. Laura was not at all well. She was struggling with her knees and obviously in a considerable amount of pain. In this country we hear of people suffering waiting for operations, but at least they live in relative comfort. To be struggling as Laura was in an environment with no comforts must have been extremely difficult and painful. She was to die shortly after my visit. She had lived to an age beyond which few Kenyans survive. She had seen many changes during her lifetime and produced several children, three of whom I had sponsored at various times.[15] If there had been no language barrier, I am sure she could have told me some very interesting stories.

Due to the unplanned nature of this visit, I spent some time amusing myself. Apart from visiting the schools and the women, there was not a great deal that I could achieve. The most inconvenient problem that I experienced on this visit was a bout of constipation. I do not eat vast quantities of food in the heat, but I was most likely not drinking enough. Although there were copious supplies of water which Benedict replenished regularly in his freezer, if not drunk promptly, the water soon warmed up and became less appetising. It was important to carry water at all times, but it was not difficult to neglect the fact that it was there to be consumed at regular intervals. Bosco escorted me to the dispensary, where one of the Sisters presented me with a bottle of what she called "liquid paraffin". The mind boggled! To me, paraffin served one purpose and that was to be ignited. I was hoping that on this occasion I was not about to be expected to ignite anything! My anxieties were laid to rest when I discovered that, in fact, the substance was actually castor oil. I remained a little dubious, having never actually consumed such a substance previously, but I was assured that it would have little effect other than to relieve my problem. It did not require any great intelligence to ascertain how it was supposed to work. Whether it was a psychological or a physical cure, I have no idea, but it had the desired effect!

As my visit approached its conclusion, I was delighted with the way in which events appeared to be unfolding. Albert had completed his secondary school with results that would be sufficient to earn him a position at any university in the country. I decided to fund a short computer course for him, which would assist him in his studies. As it was to turn out, Albert's main problem was unrelated to his academic achievements. He had no birth certificate! It is amazing the obstacles that need to be surmounted when confronted with the offspring of people

---

[15] One, Angelo, was sponsored only briefly as he was less ambitious than his siblings.

who are essentially nomads. Registering a child's birth was not high on the list of priorities of these people. Lacking a birth certificate was no barrier to advancement at primary or secondary school, but once one ventured beyond the confines of Loiyangalani, it became mandatory. Obtaining such a document proved to be anything but straightforward, necessitating various costly trips to Marsabit. Once obtained, it was sufficient to ensure enrolment at Moi University in Eldoret in a course of 'Actuarial Science'. If I had been asked what course I had expected Albert to select, I doubt that this particular course would have featured on any shortlist. Quite why it was chosen, I was never to discover, as decisions were made once I had returned to England.

One of the final tasks was to ensure that arrangements were in place for the students who were to attend secondary school the following year should they attain the desired results at primary school. At this time, the charity had been responsible for about ten students, but the response in England had been such that sponsors had been recruited to sponsor at least an additional ten. At present, those being sponsored attended a variety of schools because of the problems at the local secondary school. It had fallen on Bosco's shoulders to ensure that fees were paid, travel arrangements organised, and any additional items purchased so that the students were suitably prepared for the schooling. I was acutely aware of the burden being placed with Bosco and was keen not to increase his workload greatly. It must be remembered that the nearest bank was in Marsabit and internet banking was, as yet, not an option. As a result, we decided that the majority of the new students should attend the Loiyangalani Secondary School. I had my reservations at the time, but was assured that plans to upgrade the school were well underway and that the problems should be resolved in the not-too-distant future. As it happened, these reassurances were misdirected! This decision was to lead to problems that had to be resolved on my subsequent visit.

Monday, 25th February 2013 dawned just like any other day; the day of my departure! I spent much of the morning saying my goodbyes. The scheduled departure time was lunchtime, but as had often been the case on previous journeys, this particular moment passed without any sign of the arrival of a suitable mode of transport at Palm Shade Camp. I was not unduly perturbed. My destination was Marsabit as I had booked a flight with MAF from Marsabit to Nairobi. I had decided that I was permitted some luxury after having endured so much discomfort on my previous journeys to and from Loiyangalani. This flight was leaving at about 1 pm the following day, Tuesday; I would then be in plenty of time for the flight home from Nairobi Airport, which was scheduled for the Wednesday evening. I realised that Bosco had planned to travel via South Horr, as we had the headmaster from one of the local schools wishing to alight there. However, I had factored this into my schedule, so was not unduly concerned.

As it happened, being at the camp for lunch ensured that I would receive some sustenance, for which I was actually to feel most grateful considering the events that were about to unfold. At about 4.30 pm the vehicle finally turned up. Bosco explained that the vehicle had been delayed due to a mechanical problem. Was that an ominous warning? Should I have aborted my trip at that point? Bosco assured me that the driver was a mechanic, so should anything untoward happen, we were in safe hands. I had no idea as to the nature of the problem (or problems!), but given what was to follow, it could well have been a combination of issues and I am certain that most mechanics would have declared the vehicle unsuitable for travelling any significant distance. Having no knowledge of Swahili, I could not ascertain the content of any conversation between Bosco and the mechanic. By the time the vehicle was loaded with luggage and passengers, we finally rolled out of Palm Shade Camp at 5 pm. I was assigned a seat in the front, which I considered to be most fortunate until I was informed that the door to the passenger seat could only be opened from the outside! Hopefully, there would be no requirement for an emergency exit! Amongst the passengers were both Albert and Bonke, another student whose education we had assisted with.

Before we had reached the escarpment, we experienced the first puncture. While the wheel was being changed, a vehicle stopped to ask us if we were all right. Optimistically, we replied that we were fine; as it turned out, before we reached South Horr we were to experience transmission problems, fuel problems and electrical problems, the last of which became acutely significant given that it had become dark. Driving without headlights was not an option. The vehicle had also decided not to start each time it came to a halt. This necessitated jump-starting it. Given that the terrain was often sandy, the road was not straight and the driver was not that proficient at jump-starting anything, this was to prove a real handicap. In fact, the driving skills of the driver left a lot to be desired, even by Kenyan standards! He seemed to have a distinct reluctance to 'rev' the motor. He continually moved up the gears when the engine 'revs' were significantly lower than they should have been, which introduced a susceptibility to stalling. We limped into South Horr at midnight. The journey had taken seven instead of the usual four hours. I think the headmaster was extremely relieved at not having to travel any further!

Despite the lateness of the hour, we visited Nyeri Boys' School, as I had gifts for the boys we were sponsoring. This was the second year in a row that they had been summoned at night in order to accept gifts from their sponsors. On this occasion, they had actually been asleep and had had to be roused from their slumber by the night watchman! Surely, they must have wondered why we could not arrange to visit them at a more convenient time! There were, after all, plenty of daylight hours! They put on brave faces and managed to be suitably grateful for the gifts, despite the lateness of the hour. We were given supper somewhere in the village. I recorded in my diary that this consisted of two hard-boiled eggs, an orange and a piece of unidentified fruit! One had to be thankful for small mercies, or should one say 'offerings'?

We moved on from South Horr to resume our journey to Marsabit. Despite the inconvenience of the delays, there remained sufficient time to reach our destination before my flight south, as the journey usually takes about six hours and we were driving through the night.

To say that it was an eventful night would be an understatement. I lost count of the number of times that we were forced to stop during the remainder of the night. Fuel seemed to be reluctant to travel from the tank to the engine, so necessitated further stoppages. We had at least two punctures. Given that the supply of spare tyres had by now been exhausted, inner tubes had to be repaired in order to become inflatable. Yes, we are talking about an era when inner tubes were very much in evidence! A 'repair' required the location of the puncture, the application of a patch, the reinsertion of the inner tube into the tyre and then the inflation of the tyre using a foot pump, a process that would often take more than thirty minutes. As mentioned, the ignition system had long since decided not to cooperate and so more pushing was required. On one or two occasions, the vehicle had to be pushed a significant distance in order to find a stretch of road suitable for a jump-start. At times, the procedure would fail, so the vehicle had to be pushed back to where the process had commenced in order to initiate another attempt. Given the less than adequate driving skills of the driver, repeating the procedure was a regular occurrence.

Due to the number of occasions that we were forced to stop, I was able to verify that either the solar system or the earth was moving! The location of the various constellations altered each time I was able to observe them. Over the course of the night, I was able to confirm the complete transit of some of them from one side of the night sky to the other. At least there was something to observe – and what a picture at that!

By the time that the sun had started to rise, I was beginning to wonder if the vehicle would ever reach its destination. On one occasion, the mechanic was endeavouring to provide a solution to the constant problem regarding the fuel, when I observed some very ominous-looking tracks in the dirt beside the road. "Simba!" one of the passengers exclaimed. My knowledge of Swahili was not brilliant, but that was one word I did understand. I had been unaware that lions patrolled this particular area. I was informed that they were few and far between and only sighted on rare occasions. I stared at the bushes, wondering whether we were being observed. Eventually, the mechanic stated that he believed that the fuel problem had been rectified. This was comforting, but Marsabit still appeared to be light years away from our location. We had made very little progress during the hours of darkness. My chances of boarding the plane to Nairobi appeared to be diminishing by the minute. Nevertheless, after the obligatory push, the motor burst into life and we were on our way.

For a short while, we made good progress. We passed a vehicle travelling in the opposite direction that appeared to be loaded with uniformed personnel. We were asked if we were all right. An affirmative response was not the one that I would have given, but perhaps the sight of uniforms elicited an element of fear, so the opportunity for any meaningful assistance disappeared in a cloud of dust, literally! We then had yet another puncture. By now, the sun was up and it had become quite hot. The only shade was a small patch of ground at the front of the vehicle, into which I positioned myself, grateful for any protection from the heat. Unfortunately, the patch was shrinking more rapidly than the rate at which the puncture was being fixed. I remember thinking about my work colleagues sitting in their comfortable office back in England. For the vast majority of time, no matter what I was doing, even being squashed in the rear of a vehicle, I always considered being in Kenya to be preferable to being at my desk in the office doing the mundane tasks that were expected of me at work. This was the only occasion that I can recall when I considered that the safety of the office was preferable to being broken down in a hot, dry desert with little prospect of significant progress. Eventually, we clambered back into the vehicle to progress a few more metres. In fact, that was exactly what it was. The next puncture followed very soon afterwards. It became apparent that we were not experiencing additional punctures; it was the patches on one particular inner tube were failing. This inner tube had been repaired so many times that the repairs were not sufficient to withstand the forces to which they were subjected travelling along the road.

Finally, the vehicle ground to a halt yet again in the middle of nowhere and the mechanic announced that nothing could be done. The vehicle could not progress any further without a new inner tube. Joy of joys, what was to be done? We could await the passing of another vehicle, but we had only seen two in twenty-four hours, so the wait could be extensive. There was no phone signal, so we could not phone for assistance. By this time, I had long since realised that the plane from Marsabit would depart without me, which would necessitate a complete reorganisation of my plans to reach Nairobi, all of which seemed more than slightly insignificant given that we remained a considerable distance from Marsabit with no apparent means of progressing.

I knew that there was a small village called Kargi some distance this side of Marsabit, as we had passed through it on a previous trip. We had been on the road for a considerable amount of time, so I surmised it had to be relatively close. After some discussion, it was decided that it was probably no more than ten kilometres ahead. I decided somewhat rashly that, if that was the case, some of us should attempt to walk there. Not wishing to remain in a static vehicle, and being a reasonable walker, I proclaimed that I was happy to be included in the walking party. If the estimated distance was anywhere near the correct one, we should at least be able to see the village after walking for an hour or so, and that was infinitely preferable to being confined to a stationary vehicle at the mercy of the hot sun. As a result, Bosco, Bonke, Albert and I set off at a reasonable pace full of what could only be termed as misplaced confidence. We made good progress despite the heat. After about fifty minutes, with no obvious change in the scenery, I was beginning to doubt the accuracy of the estimates regarding the distance to Kargi. Having travelled along the road previously, I knew a small range of hills should be visible for about two kilometres on the approach to the village. There was no sign of these hills and so the distance had been a considerable underestimation.

I was becoming weary and needed a drink, so it was decided that Bosco and Albert would endeavour to keep walking while Bonke and I waited beside the road. We found an acacia tree that provided some shade, sat down and waited. I did make a quick inspection before sitting down to ensure that no undesirable creepy-crawlies had also decided that this particular tree would be a good place to rest during the midday sun. It also occurred to me that Bonke and I were probably the only two people ever to have sat under this particular tree as it had no distinguishing features that would have made it a chosen location for anyone else. It just happened to be close to where I had decided that enough was enough. Quite what I expected to happen next and how long I had anticipated having to sit there, I simply do not know. Bonke and I did ponder as to from which direction help would eventually emerge. We had no doubt that it would! We looked longing in the direction into which Albert and Bosco had disappeared. You can imagine our surprise when we could hear a vehicle apparently limping, if vehicles could be described as limping, coming from the other direction. Was this ability to break down catching? Had some other vehicle experienced problems and was only now desperately trying to reach Kargi? No, it was our vehicle! A miracle had occurred! An apparently undrivable vehicle had become mobile! It turned out that the mechanic had decided to fill the tyre that required an inner tube with deflated inner tubes in such a way that it was sufficiently padded to give enough support to the tyre so that by driving gingerly progress could be made, albeit comparatively slowly.

We climbed aboard and resumed the journey to Kargi. The vehicle was moving at little more than walking pace, but it was not long before we came across Albert and Bosco still walking. With no obvious indication as to the proximity of the village, they were most relieved to be reunited with the vehicle. As it happened, the ten kilometres had been a gross underestimation of the distance to Kargi. It was likely to have been greater than ten *miles* when we set off. Eventually the hills and then the village appeared, and there was great rejoicing. We had reached a destination of sorts, and help would be at hand. Unfortunately, the vehicle had one last trick up its sleeve. With our destination within touching distance, there was a resounding thud. One end of the crankshaft had come adrift and deposited itself on to the road. With my patience severely strained, and desperate for a drink, I was released from

112

the vehicle and headed towards the village convinced that I would never set foot inside that wretched vehicle again. On reaching a premise that served cool drinks in the company of Albert and Bonke, I purchased fizzy drinks for the three of us, the contents of which were consumed in such a manner that they literally 'never touched the sides'. Shortly after, we were joined by other members of our party, including Bosco. We also managed to procure cold water, which enabled us to consider our next move.

As mentioned above, I was aware that the MAF flight from Marsabit to Nairobi would have departed without one of its passengers. I was to discover later that they had been very concerned as to what fate may have befallen me, given my failure not only to board the plane but also to have contacted them with some reason for my non-attendance. Obviously, notification from the middle of a desert had been impossible, except possibly by a carrier pigeon if it had not succumbed to the heat or been devoured by some hungry bird of prey.

It was now late afternoon on the Tuesday. I had failed to reach Marsabit. My only mode of transport had died, and I had an international flight to catch on Wednesday. Things were not looking good, and Bosco had no solution. The only other vehicle in Kargi destined for Marsabit had also broken down and was awaiting a spare part to arrive from Marsabit. Bosco assured me that he would keep me informed as to any developments. At present, he had to oversee repairs to his vehicle.

Bonke, Albert and I walked to the mission buildings in the hope that the Consolata Fathers, who seemed to be everywhere, might have a plan. As it happened, they were away. With nothing to be done, we found shady spots on a concrete floor and managed to have a much-needed snooze. I dared not contemplate the ensuing possibilities, but at least we had reached civilisation!

Despite Kargi being some distance from Loiyangalani, families knew each other. Bonke took me to a friend's house. He very kindly cooked me some chapatis. It is amazing what one finds in the remotest of places. The young man had a small tin of tomato concentrate. I had no idea how long it had been sitting in his larder or from where it had originated, but the contents added excellent flavour to the chapatis! He had very little to offer me in the way of cold drink. He did have a bottle of ginger beer, which Kenyans apparently distribute only for medicinal purposes as a cure for stomach ailments. The two lads were therefore highly amused when I remarked that I would very much like to consume the drink, even though I had no stomach ailments of which I was aware. We did also enjoy copious cups of *chai*. Once the ginger beer had been consumed, I was loath to sample the local water, so the *chai* appeared to be a safer option with which to quench my thirst.

With the arrival of darkness, I decided to challenge Bosco as to possible plans. It turned out that the part for the alternative vehicle had arrived from Marsabit and repairs were to be undertaken through the night. It also appeared that the damage to Bosco's vehicle was not as serious as it had at first seemed. There was, therefore, something of a race developing to see which vehicle would be the first to emerge as being roadworthy. Around midnight, it seemed that I would be travelling to Marsabit in the alternative vehicle. Just as I was about to opt for this plan, Bosco informed me that I would then have to make my own way to Nairobi, which could leave me little time to catch my flight. He continued by saying that his vehicle was almost ready and he had an alternative plan that could shorten my journey considerably and would involve bypassing Marsabit.

The plan was to drive through the night via a small village called Korr. We would then take a road heading towards Laisamis. I would be deposited at a bus stop from which I could proceed on my journey south, saving a considerable amount of time. This left me in a quandary. Was I to travel in a vehicle that was probably the more reliable of the two in order to reach Marsabit, from which I would have some distance to travel? Was I to trust Bosco's statement that his vehicle was indeed now roadworthy, despite the fact that it had so far proved to be distinctly unreliable? There was no doubt that Bosco appreciated the urgency of my situation and would obviously do all he could to ensure that I did not miss my international flight.

I decided to remain with Bosco and his vehicle. His optimism was infectious, although I could not understand how the repairs could have been accomplished in an environment that was far from mechanically accommodating. It was at about 2 am on Wednesday morning that we set off on the next stage of the journey. It took just over an hour to reach Korr without having had any breakdowns. This seemed too good to be true. Perhaps my troubles were over. Upon reaching Korr, however, we encountered a small problem. No one knew the correct road to our destination, which was, in fact, a small village south of Laisamis called Merille.

Shortly after 3 am, we stopped outside a house in Korr that had been selected at random. After much pounding on the door, the occupant was roused from his slumber. He was asked if he could show us the road that we needed for Merille. He boarded our vehicle, directing us through the village, which was considerably larger than I had expected. Once it became apparent that we were on the correct road, he was unceremoniously dumped by the side of the road in order to find his way home. He had been most happy to have been of assistance and waved to us with a smile on his face. The whole scenario was quite extraordinary. This was not something that one would do in England, although I had on one occasion asked directions from one poor householder rousing her from her slumber in the early hours of the morning, having become hopelessly lost due to diversions caused by an excessive snowstorm in England. At least on that occasion, she did not have to accompany me in the car only to be dumped on the side of the road in the freezing cold once I had reached my destination.

Unfortunately, our troubles were far from over. Having left Korr, we found ourselves on a very sandy road with mountains on either side. It was at this point that the vehicle decided to commence its familiar pattern of breakdowns. At least we had no more punctures! However, finding a straight piece of road along which to push the vehicle became problematic, with the sand ensuring that the pushing required greater effort than had been the case for our earlier breakdowns. Frustratingly, on more than one occasion, I believe the stalling of the engine had not been caused by a genuine breakdown but by the driver's tendency to change gear without revving the engine sufficiently. As morning approached, I noted in my diary that "just before dawn I became very despondent". As far as I was concerned, I had no idea where we were, with visions of yet another plane leaving without one of its passengers.

As the occupants of the vehicle, including in all probability the driver, were becoming wearier, I decided to become proactive. Each time the driver attempted to change gear too early, I told him to refrain from doing so until I perceived the engine to be revving sufficiently to allow a gear change. In retrospect, I should have interceded much earlier, as this had the desired effect with the cessation of breakdowns. By now it was daylight, which helped the driver. I had mentioned earlier that we had had electrical problems and the headlights had been less successful at guiding us than they should have been. Being able to see exactly where one was going was certainly helpful!

At last, civilisation! Having reached Merille, the start of the tarmac road could be seen. After refreshments but no food, I parted company with my friends. They had been bound for Marsabit, diverting solely to ensure that I could catch my plane. They were not too far south of their intended objective. Provided that their driver managed to drive sensibly, I am sure they would have reached their destination before me.

I did have two fellow travellers who were to remain with me until I reached Nairobi. The three of us boarded a bus destined for Isiolo, but unbelievably, this too had a puncture, and we were asked to change vehicles before reaching our destination. Once in Isiolo, there was again no time to pause for refreshments. I had to commandeer sole use, with my two companions, of a *matatu*, to ensure that we could arrive in Nairobi without incurring a multitude of halts to collect or deposit passengers. I am not sure what instructions had been conveyed to the driver, but he proceeded like a bat out of hell. At times, I simply clung on and closed my eyes. We did stop once. You have guessed it; we had another puncture! It seemed that no matter in which particular vehicle I was to travel on this particular journey, I was to be afflicted by the dreaded puncture ailment! Changing a wheel rather than repairing a puncture ensured that the stop was very brief, and we soon resumed our dash to Nairobi with the minimum of fuss. We arrived in Nairobi at 3.15 pm, something that I could not have believed possible at various stages during the last two days, especially as dawn had unfolded on that particular morning.

My two companions ensured that I was safely ensconced in a taxi to return me to the Consolata mission before bidding me farewell. Upon returning to the mission, I shed the clothes that had accumulated vast quantities of dust and dirt. I then participated in a lengthy shower. Feeling like a new man, I then ventured across to the local market, where I purchased a melon, a mango and some passion fruit, all of which I conveyed to the dining room in the mission. Fruit in Kenya is always special. It is always ready to eat. On this occasion, these few pieces of fruit could only be described as nectar. I had had very little to eat since leaving Loiyangalani, and what I had eaten had been bizarre. To say that these few pieces of fruit were the most satisfying pieces of fruit that I have ever consumed would not be an exaggeration.

Later that evening, I had supper at the mission, and Father Joya kindly drove me to the airport in plenty of time to catch the plane that I had genuinely believed at one stage would leave without me. He had been alarmed to have been informed that I was not on my scheduled flight from Marsabit, as he had been prepared to collect me from that airport, but he was amused by the details of my journey.

I do look upon this particular journey as something quite extraordinary. Bosco's vehicle was in no fit state to undertake such a venture. I was very fortunate that he had found a mechanic who appeared to have been able to solve every mechanical challenge that had arisen. As far as I know, these challenges had been met solely by improvisation. I cannot believe that he had managed to acquire any significant replacement parts in Kargi. Bosco was a good friend. I am sure he was very embarrassed by all that happened, but I am equally certain that his vehicle was probably the only one available to make the trip at that time. We were travelling through very hostile terrain, so the situation could have become far worse had any of the breakdowns proved terminal. The roads are used by other travellers, so becoming stranded for an excessive period of time was probably most unlikely. It was my concern regarding the international flight that spurred Bosco to make the decisions that he did. Without that worry, he most likely would have remained in Kargi for a day or two, possibly hitching a ride to Marsabit to collect any spare parts. As is said, 'all's well that ends well'.

CHAPTER EIGHT

A Poignant Farewell

My next trip to Loiyangalani was in February 2014. The chair of our committee decided that she would like to visit Loiyangalani for the second time. There were three other interested persons, making a total of five.

The flight from England to Nairobi via Dubai was identical to that used on previous visits. However, on this occasion, the ladies' luggage managed to absent itself from our flight, much to the consternation of all concerned upon arriving in Nairobi. As was his custom, Father Joya ensured that he was present at the airport to collect us. The ladies were understandably concerned about the whereabouts of their luggage, and so the greeting was somewhat muted. As it happened, the luggage arrived on the following flight, necessitating another tedious trip to the airport to reunite it with its owners.

The following day, the ever-dependable Father Joya kindly drove us to Wilson Airport for our internal flight. His willingness to assist us in our travels was something that I have greatly appreciated over the years. We had managed to book a flight destined for Lodwar, which is on the western side of Lake Turkana. MAF were happy to incorporate a small diversion to enable us to land at Loiyangalani en route. This was extremely helpful, as the visit was short and time spent on the road to and from Marsabit would have eaten into our stay at Loiyangalani. The flight path was due west of our previous route, and so we were treated to stunning views of the Rift Valley. As usual, it was extremely windy on our approach to the Loiyangalani airstrip, which is rarely used. This necessitated an 'inspection' sweep over the landing zone (one could scarcely think of it as a runway!). The pilot wanted to judge the possible effects that the side wind might have on his landing, but he also wished to ensure that any unsuspecting animals, or indeed humans, had vacated the area before attempting the landing. Apparently, the locals were slightly bemused, wondering why the landing appeared to have been aborted on the first sweep, thinking that perhaps we had decided to go elsewhere. The rarity of planes in the area had ensured an impressive welcoming committee. It was evidently an event not to be missed.

We were escorted to Palm Shade Camp with no lack of volunteers eager to assist us with our luggage. Benedict gave us time to settle in before offering us lunch. It was to be a leisurely start to our visit. I had scarcely finished my lunch when Albert arrived to inform me that Raphael, whom I was sponsoring, was feeling unwell. I accompanied Albert to Raphael's hut to find him complaining of a stomach problem. We escorted him to the Dispensary, where we were met by one of the Consolata Sisters. Despite this visit being out of hours, the Sisters are always most accommodating. Raphael was examined and a diagnosis was made. As the conversation was in Swahili, I had no idea as to the problem. Medicine was produced for which I had to pay a small fee. Raphael soon recovered. I wish all medical problems could be solved so easily. I think the situation had arisen from the fact that Raphael did not have the money to procure any medicine, hence the situation having become 'more severe' upon my arrival. I am not sure that his illness could in any way have been described as life-threatening!

Upon my return to Palm Shade Camp, I discovered that a deputation of secondary school students whom we had commenced sponsoring last year had arrived. They were attending the Loiyangalani Secondary School as a result of my previous decision that we should support the school. Despite the fact that Albert had managed to obtain a reasonable grade, the school was not catering for the needs of its students. Two years ago, we had been most concerned about the school, but my visit last year had led me to believe that the situation was improving. The students had also appeared contented. Over the past twelve months, it appeared that the situation had deteriorated significantly. There was a list of complaints ranging from poor teaching to bad organisation and a general lack of resources. In short, the students not only considered that our money was being wasted but that they had little hope of achieving satisfactory results. I had had my doubts about the school since its inception, but I had no idea that factors had conspired to such an extent that feelings amongst the students were so raw. At that stage there was little we could do, so we promised to visit the school on the following day and discuss the situation with the headmaster and the other members of staff. We realised that issues needed to be addressed and decisions taken before we departed. It appears that matters had come to a head only recently, which was why Bosco had been unable to warn us in advance.

In the early evening, we ventured into the settlement to the south of the village. As before, the young children were delighted to accompany us, clinging to any available white hand. Despite the shrieks of delight from the children, there was always a sense of tranquillity as the sun disappeared behind the western shore of the lake. This was a scene that had occurred every day for countless thousands of years before Loiyangalani had become a settlement of any description. I have wondered how many of the Rendille tribesman who frequented the area before it was settled stopped to admire the sunset at this particular point. They could never have contemplated the changes that would take place once the first white explorers had visited the lake just over a hundred years ago. Observing the first caravan arrive at the end of the nineteenth century would have been a considerable shock to any local tribesman accustomed to his nomadic existence, undisturbed apart from the threat posed by some of his belligerent neighbours.

The following morning, Benedict drove us round the village for the benefit of the three members of the party who had not previously visited the area. Benedict's vehicle turned out to be considerably more reliable than that owned by Bosco on my previous visit. I had been loath to ask Bosco what had become of his vehicle, but there was little evidence of its existence while we were in Loiyangalani. Perhaps he had decided that he was better off without it.

We had been invited to meet the District Commissioner. Even after our visit and having listened to him speak, we were none the wiser as to the precise nature of his role. He obviously regarded himself as being very important in the grand scheme of things. He had a very elaborate and lavishly furnished office in a building that was set apart from all other buildings in the area, as if to emphasise its importance. He was very smartly dressed, which contrasted sharply with the attire that we were wearing. Nevertheless, he was keen to know our plans and was quick to thank us for all that we were doing. We had been warned to be on our best behaviour and not to ask any question that might ruffle any feathers! It appeared that the ramifications of any controversial questions may have caused problems for our friends once we had left. I believe that we passed the test with flying colours, as our host was very amicable when we departed.

Benedict then continued the tour by taking us to El Molo for a brief visit. Again, basket-ware was purchased, this time as souvenirs rather than to sell. We then returned to Palm Shade Camp for lunch.

After lunch, we embarked upon the promised visit to the secondary school. There was no doubt that there had been yet more deterioration in the state of the buildings. The incomplete science building appeared to have become *more* incomplete, in that sections that were present last year seemed to have since disappeared. Whether locals had helped themselves to what they perceived to be potential building materials or whether parts had simply disintegrated, I do not know. A hole of considerable size was rapidly expanding in the roof, and the computer equipment remained securely boxed in another building. Upon discussing the situation with the teachers, it also became apparent that there remained an insufficient number of teachers to ensure that each subject in the school curriculum was covered to the desired level. Morale was low amongst students and staff. Again, we were promised that the situation would improve. There had been a high turnover of staff, but some of the new teachers were determined to initiate change.

We had been informed that there were a limited number of places available at Nyero Boys' School in South Horr, the school that had been the subject of our nocturnal visits on previous occasions! As I was sponsoring Raphael, I decided that he should move forthwith, exactly what he was hoping! He was intelligent and clearly frustrated, not only by the lack of facilities at Loiyangalani Secondary School but also by the fact that he felt that he would never optimise his chances of obtaining the grades he required to progress. Nyero Boys' School was more expensive, and so careful consideration was needed regarding our resources and whether we had the financial wherewithal to finance moving all the students. Moving students would require additional funds from sponsors. As it happened, some of the students did not wish to move; they were asking for pledges from the hierarchy in the school that improvements would be forthcoming. They were hoping that our presence would galvanise the headteacher and his staff into action. Removing each of our students would send a very negative message to the people of Loiyangalani. It was important to reach some sort of compromise whereby we could be seen to support the school in some way. It is not

121

easy treading the tightrope between diplomacy and the interests of the students.

As outsiders, our reactions were being observed by the local community. There is a very fine line between being destructive and constructive. If students, especially the brighter ones, are removed from the school, its results will never attain a satisfactory standard. If it is not seen as successful, the number of attendees will diminish and so initiate a downward spiral. However, each individual has one and only one opportunity to attain grades that can ensure a promising future. I, for one, if I invest my funds in a student, wish the chances of success for that student to be optimised.

Once Raphael had been moved, his results improved rapidly. He never looked back. He went to university and attained a good degree, all of which may have proved impossible had he remained at the Loiyangalani Secondary School. Our actions were to bring about a gradual change. Although the school does not cater for the very bright students who continue to attend other schools, standards have improved and a significant number of students, especially those who wish to remain close to their families, are happy to attend the school.

Upon our return, Bosco introduced us to the primary school students who had been selected for sponsorship in the following year should they achieve the grades expected from them. This entailed further discussion as to the suitability of Loiyangalani Secondary School, but Bosco advised us to wait before making any decisions as he was confident that the situation would improve. He did also point out that if he was seen to be directing students away from the local secondary school, this would be to his detriment in the community. Life is never straightforward. Many factors have to be taken into consideration when making any decision.

We were glad to be able to relax in the evening with another visit to the area south of the village, not only to view the sunset, but also to meet the families of the students we had just met with Bosco. Once the families had realised that we intended to help their children, the outpouring of blessings and thanks was incredible. Again and again, it was becoming obvious that by spending relatively small sums of money, it was so easy to change the lives and prospects of individuals. The appreciation shown by these families was, at times, overwhelming and very difficult to respond to.

Over the first two days of our visit, we attracted the attention of a rather corpulent priest, Father Raymond, from Kargi, who happened to be visiting Loiyangalani. The reason for his visit was never to be revealed. He appeared to be in no hurry to return to Kargi. He had the very useful knack of appearing at Palm Shade Camp just as our meal was being prepared. Being the friendly lot that we are, we could not consume a meal without inviting him to participate, an invitation that he never declined. Our presence in the dining area had a tendency to attract various people, but none were quite so consistent in their attendance as this very friendly priest. He was very good company and did promise to take us to South Horr, which was most kind. Although this gesture was part of a pre-planned excursion, it was greatly appreciated.

After breakfast the following day, we prepared ourselves for the journey. Father Raymond arrived with the vehicle and a driver. He turned out to be a very interesting guide, so our generosity with the meals was well rewarded. We made a few stops along the way. The inhabitants of one enterprising small village, Sarima, had started cultivating bananas. The project was in its infancy, so I have no idea whether it was to be a success. I had my doubts, as the supply of water was very inconsistent.

We arrived in South Horr without any unforeseen problems of a mechanical nature, which was a relief. We visited Nyero Girls' School. The corresponding boys' school was well established and much in demand, so it had been decided to build a girls' school in the village. It was interesting that the secondary schools seemed to be single sex. The fundamental reason for this related to the necessity to board. It was deemed easier to limit the boarding facilities to one sex. Although the girls' school appeared to have excellent facilities and we were to support it by nominating one or two of our students to attend, initially it was to suffer a similar fate to that of the Loiyangalani Secondary School. More than one single sex girls' school with very satisfactory results already existed in the area and there was little demand for another. The school failed to attract bright students and outstanding staff, so within a year we had to reassign the girls that we had sent to this school to other schools. Eventually, the school was to recover, with the introduction of well-motivated staff who displayed the dedication required to ensure the students attained satisfactory grades.

From there, we visited the Nyero Boys' School. Despite having been there twice before, I had never arrived in daylight, so it was a joy to be able to look round the school. I think the boys we were sponsoring were relieved not to have to be dragged out of their beds in order to show their appreciation for what we were doing. The headmaster escorted us around the school and encouraged us to continue sending our students there. He confirmed the notion that the payment of fees from students who are sponsored was more consistent than fees from those who are not. Although the school appeared to be sound financially, I believe that the cash flow could become a problem if the payment of fees was sporadic, arriving only when a student was about to be ejected from the school. On one occasion, our payment was delayed for various reasons, but it caused no more than mild aggravation as the headmaster had sufficient trust in our organisation to realise it was only a temporary glitch.

Having consolidated our relationship with this school, we visited the premises of the company that was to establish a wind farm of three hundred and sixty-five wind turbines within five years. The site for this project was to be an area between South Horr and Loiyangalani. I was sceptical, having heard about well-meaning projects that failed to eventuate. This one seemed incredible. Before building any turbines, a road would have to be constructed. The logistics were mind-boggling. As it happens, the project was to be completed on time.

Our return journey to Loiyangalani necessitated further pauses for the collection of passengers and cargo! Despite its protestations, a live goat, which had been deposited in a sack with only its head protruding, was tied on to the roof rack. It was obviously not impressed with its surroundings because it could be heard complaining most of the way to Loiyangalani. At one stage it decided to show its displeasure by urinating. Fortunately, the window down which the urine flowed was actually closed at the time, as it could have been a rather unpleasant experience for the poor unfortunate passenger sitting adjacent to the window. Needless to say, it was dark by the time we returned to Loiyangalani. Very few journeys seemed to commence or terminate on schedule, but no one was in any hurry, so it really did not matter. I think we were all relieved to be able to disembark and distance ourselves from the poor goat. As it happens, the goat did not appear to have suffered greatly from its ordeal. It was probably happy to once again be on *terra firma*, but as it was most likely destined for the pot, it would have been safer back on the roof of the vehicle. At least it had not suffered from travel sickness! The ever-dependable Benedict had supper waiting for us. The poor man never knew exactly when we would be turning up for meals, but the food was always well-prepared and ready to eat.

The following morning, we again visited the primary school. We were treated to another fine display of singing, dancing and poetry-reading.

There is no doubt that the children greatly enjoy the opportunity to perform. They were permitted to wear tribal costumes. The girls especially went to great lengths to adorn themselves with a variety of necklaces and bracelets of all colours, except pink! I am certain that being asked to wear tribal attire gave them a huge sense of pride. It is easy to stereotype girls and boys, but there is no doubt that the girls showed less in the way of inhibitions, becoming so involved in what they were doing that they could have been in another world. They are naturally more fluent and graceful than the boys. It was a joy to watch them. The students of both sexes were keen to show how much they appreciated what we were doing for them. A special song had been composed for the occasion, fortunately sung in English so that we could understand the content.

We again had lunch at Palm Shade Camp. Benedict was determined to ensure that we were never hungry, but I do not eat a great deal in the heat, so was not always able to show my appreciation in the same way that I would have done in England. While we were eating, I was alerted to the presence of two very special visitors. Albert's parents were true nomads who lived in the desert country with their goats. They knew I had financed their son's education and were determined to show their gratitude. Word had somehow been conveyed to them regarding my visit. They embarked on a journey which required a trek of twenty-five kilometres in each direction in order to present me with a goat. This was the first time that anyone in any country had presented me with a live goat – and will probably the last. I was deeply moved by the generosity of this gesture. We sat down and conducted a conversation of sorts, with Albert doing the translation. All I could give them in return was a Coca Cola, but they seemed to be very grateful for that. As they wished to complete the return journey before dark, they did not stay for too long. I am not sure whether they knew what I would do with the goat, but I am certain Albert would have explained. Although we had managed to transport a goat on the roof of a vehicle, there was little doubt that this particular animal would be going nowhere. Imagine turning up at Nairobi Airport with a live goat asking for it to be shipped back to England! Quite what I would have done with it had it ever managed to negotiate the various hurdles required for the importation of livestock, I do not know. I am certain my dog would have enjoyed chasing it round my comparatively small garden!

As it happened, this was our last evening and we were entertaining the primary school teachers for supper, so the goat was a welcome addition to the pot! The poor goat was duly despatched and became a part of the feast. It was greatly appreciated by the teachers. Although not my favourite food, I was able to consume an amount that was significant enough to show my gratitude for the gift. The goat still remains one of the most, if not *the* most, memorable gift that I have ever received. Over the years, I have been the recipient of many gifts and presents from people who have been both thoughtful and generous, but I have never received anything like this, given from the heart and necessitating such an arduous journey for its delivery. Describing the experience as truly magical fails to do it justice.

After a relatively quiet afternoon, the evening was very sociable, but the combination of sun and wind ensures that one is easily fatigued. Lack of sleep at night is an additional factor in the constant battle to remain alert during the day and the early part of the evening when one is doing one's utmost to entertain friends.

The final day in Loiyangalani commenced with another visit to the dispensary for the obligatory dose of "liquid paraffin". My previous digestive ailment had re-emerged and was remedied with the same medicinal compound that had been provided upon my previous visit.

We were then invited to visit the hut of one of the students whom we were sponsoring. On this occasion, I was permitted to enter the hut so that I could establish exactly how the interior was laid out and the nature of its contents. It was similar to entering a well-know TV doctor's time machine! From the exterior, the hut appeared quite small, but once inside, it seemed to grow in size assuming greater dimensions. There was an area for sleeping, shared by the young man, his brother and his mother. Obviously, a request for privacy of any sort by any of the inhabitants would have been extremely difficult to accommodate. There was a small dresser upon which were cups and other eating utensils. In the centre of the hut were the remains of a fire which had been used for cooking. Given the combustible nature of the building materials used in the construction of the hut, this could be classed as a distinct health and safety issue. Ventilation, apart from the entrance, was non-existent, so cooking would have necessitated a relatively smokeless fire if the chef was not to be asphyxiated by the smoke. Illumination was non-existent. Being extremely dark, it was an ideal resting place for undesirables, such as scorpions. The idea of lying down at night to have a scorpion emerge from the darkness only to crawl over one's bedding in the direction of one's face does not bear thinking about! The huts were very much a matter of pride for each individual family and great care was taken to ensure that each hut was maintained to as high a standard as possible in the circumstances. Extricating myself from the hut was nowhere near as simple as entering it. I had to emerge on hands and knees, much to the amusement of the small group of observers who had assembled to discover what was happening. Visitors from overseas were seldom, if ever, permitted to enter these huts, so I was most privileged.

I then had an important meeting with the leaders of the women's group on whose behalf I was selling the beaded items. My companions had been adamant that they would not be participants in the transportation of these artefacts to England. I had spent a considerable amount of time at weekends touring the local fairs and fetes selling the items on behalf of the women, making more money than they had ever envisaged as being possible, so they had had due reward for their labours. I did still have items to sell, so there would be more money for them. I promised that every item would be sold, although it was not to be easy selling the final few items, some of which were either too small or too large, or simply the wrong colour! Despite these difficulties, I was to fulfil my promise.

It had become obvious that the long-term future for the project was unsustainable. The women could produce items faster than I could sell them, and I could not continue to allocate the considerable amount of time necessary to ensure a constant flow of income. I had enjoyed attending the events, meeting people and explaining the nature of the venture. The precise nature of the enjoyment was very much weather-dependent. I was well-equipped with a small marquee and the necessary accessories, but operating at events when it was pouring with rain was quite a challenge, especially when it was time to dismantle everything. I hope the women could understand why I could not continue indefinitely. I trust that they have managed to find an alternative source for the sale of their wares, even if it might not be quite so lucrative.

We had lunch at Palm Shade Camp for the final time, only to discover that yet again the plane had been delayed, obviously a perennial problem! Once we had received the green light that it was in fact on its way, a sizable contingent of locals escorted us to the airstrip. There was no shortage of assistants willing to act as porters. A group of students had learnt 'Amazing Grace', which they sang in their own inimitable but most memorable way. For me, saying farewell to so many wonderful people at the same time was a very emotional experience, although it turned out that Albert had fallen asleep somewhere and consequently had missed the whole event! I was also unaware at the time that this was to be the last time I was to see Bosco. Although members of the committee were to meet him on a subsequent visit without me, very sadly he was to die of an unknown stomach illness three years later. I was never to discover the precise nature of the illness, as communication from his relatives was to be very vague. With the medical facilities in Kenya being woeful compared to those in England, the chances of a correct diagnosis were often fairly forlorn. There is no doubt that I, and the Loiyangalani Trust, owed him an enormous debt of gratitude for his dedication and energy to ensure that money was spent sensibly and that the students were able to attend their secondary schools with the minimum of fuss. Without his dedication the charity would never have managed to establish a presence in the community.

We returned safely to Wilson Airport, from where we were again collected by Father Joya. The following evening, we returned to England.

This was to be my last visit for some time. I would be sponsoring both Albert and Raphael at university over the coming years. Once Albert had completed his course, I took on another student, Damiano, who was to complete a computing degree. The chair of our committee was to continue visiting on a regular basis and there was never a shortage of volunteers wishing to accompany her. As supporting my students was not inexpensive, I decided that my resources were better spent in helping them rather than making journeys to Loiyangalani. I believe those in Loiyangalani understood the reasons behind this decision.

We were very lucky in that the man who took over the role of headmaster at Loiyangalani Primary School, Jacob, is another real gem. I have already mentioned that he used to be headmaster of the El Molo Primary School, which was very efficiently organised and grew in stature under his guidance. He has become an integral part in the continuing ability of the charity to function effectively. In fact, he has taken everything to another level of efficiency, for which we are most grateful.

CHAPTER NINE

An Unusual Christmas

It was to be seven years before my next visit to Loiyangalani. The world was in the grip of the Coronavirus pandemic; consequently, it was touch and go as to whether I would actually travel, given all the possible scenarios and restrictions. I had retired, so there were no time limits on the duration of my absence from this country. I decided that it would be a useful experience to visit Loiyangalani during the Christmas period. Christmas in the UK focuses primarily on family gatherings with copious amounts of food and drink and a liberal exchange of well-meaning gifts, all of which are appreciated but some of which are recycled as presents to friends or relations! Of course, it is also true that for many families it is a struggle to provide the food and gifts that they would so desperately wish to bestow upon their loved ones. I was, however, keen to discover the way in which Christmas is celebrated in a community in a country where significant numbers of the population live in a level of poverty that, for the vast majority of those in more affluent countries, is simply unimaginable.

It was the late summer of 2021 when I made the initial decision to visit Loiyangalani for Christmas. Coronavirus remained a major concern in both countries, but booster jabs were about to be delivered in this country and the outlook was beginning to look more positive. Life is never straightforward! As my plans were beginning to take shape, there was the emergence of a new strain of the virus, the Omicron variation. It appeared to have originated in South Africa, so that country and those to the north were hastily assigned 'red' list status, which meant isolation in draconian circumstances in hotels upon return to this country, with the general advice being, "Do not travel to these destinations." Although Kenya was not included initially, there was the worry that it would be.

Additional restrictions were imposed in the UK, with the new variant beginning to spread exponentially; there were various doom and gloom predictions, most of which turned out to be unwarranted.

As my departure date approached, I had a variety of functions which it was assumed I would attend. I had to decide whether to honour these commitments or cocoon myself at home in order to avoid any possible contact with the new virus. I decided upon the former option and thankfully managed to escape any infection, but these were a nervous few days!

As the day of my departure dawned, I realised I had probably had more tests than the prototype for Concord, more jabs than a pincushion and had had to procure more documents than a barrister in the most complex of court cases!

As it happened, the journey to Nairobi was without incident. It did take more than two hours to pass through the various stages of immigration and retrieve my baggage. I had erroneously believed that few people would be travelling, but to describe the situation in Nairobi airport as a 'bun fight' would be an understatement. Eventually, I managed to extricate myself from the terminal none the worse for wear. The next task was to locate Father Joya, who was conspicuous by his absence. Not having the means to contact him, I had to enlist the help of one of the very friendly taxi drivers, something that I had done on a previous visit. Father Joya had become confused by various diversions due to extensive roadworks in the vicinity of the airport and was grateful for the assistance from the taxi driver, who was able to guide him to the airport. It was great to see Father Joya again. He had changed very little and was undoubtedly happy to see me.

I was to stay at the Consolata Seminary in Langata where I had stayed on a previous occasion. After lunch, Father Joya took me to a nearby sports store. The Loiyangalani Trust committee had asked me to purchase various types of balls for the primary school. Whilst in the store, I was drawn to a section that was selling fireworks, not something one would find in most sports stores in the UK. I am not usually a great fan of fireworks, especially if charged with the task of endeavouring to light them and ensure that they do what they are supposed to do. Rockets can travel in a variety of directions, not necessarily vertical! On this occasion, I felt that I had been drawn to this particular section of the shop for a reason and so decided to overcome my trepidations by purchasing some rockets and some sparklers. It was only once I reached Loiyangalani that

I was to appreciate the true value and significance of this fairly mundane purchase.

The following day, Father Joya took me to Safaricom. I was able to purchase a SIM card for my mobile phone to be used whilst in Kenya. In addition, I was able to 'bank' money into the phone, which could then be used to pay for accommodation and food on my travels. It appears that credit cards are rarely, if ever, used in Kenya. The vast majority of transactions are conducted using the phone, access to which requires the use of two PIN numbers.

After lunch, Father Joya drove me into Nairobi to travel to Nyahururu by *matatu*. This was to be the first stage of my journey north. Discovering the precise location from which the *matatus* to Nyahururu actually depart required a certain amount of luck, helpful assistance from pedestrians, a friendly colleague of Father Joya's on the other end of the phone and even the aid of a policeman! Each time I have visited Nairobi over the years, I have always believed that it could never become more congested. How wrong I have been! Pedestrians can no longer use many of the pavements in the city, because the goods of various street vendors are strewn across them in front of shops that are supposedly trying to sell items of their own. Pedestrians are therefore compelled to use the road, joining whatever vehicles have the misfortune to be endeavouring to reach a destination of sorts. Added to this chaos has been the emergence of the motorbike as a means of transport. In the past, it has been the behaviour of the *matatu* drivers that has been the greatest cause for concern. They have now been regulated and behave like angels when compared to the recklessness of the motorbike riders.

Before progressing with my own journey, it is worth mentioning a few facts regarding the motorbikes. With traffic congestion in the larger towns and cities, the motorbike has become the most effective way of proceeding to one's destination. There are few, if any, regulations regarding the motorbikes or their riders. The riders are not required to take any test. The motorbikes themselves are also subject to no form of test. Often the motorbikes are purchased by individuals who then loan them to others. The riders will be paid for conveying goods or passengers, giving a proportion of their 'fares' to the owners of the motorbikes. Haste is necessary so as to maximise the amount of money that can be earnt. Most riders will weave in and out of traffic, ride on verges or pavements, overtake vehicles on their inside or outside, and generally use any means possible to ensure progress that is as swift as possible. Perhaps their most flagrant disregard for the rules of the road is best illustrated by their behaviour at some of the large roundabouts in Nairobi. In order that traffic flows reasonably smoothly, the police control the traffic at these roundabouts, to reduce the accumulation of traffic. This control appears to relate only to vehicles with four or more wheels! Motorbikes are apparently invisible, ignoring any directives, proceeding as and when they wish with total disregard for the instructions from the police, who appear to be oblivious to their presence.

For the motorbikes, there seem to be no limits to capacity. Loads are often balanced so precariously on their rear end that they resemble mobile leaning towers of Pisa! Thankfully there is little opportunity for them to travel at anything like the speeds of motorbikes in this country. However, Father Joya told me that accidents are so prolific that the injured fill a complete hospital in Nairobi. The preferred headgear seems to be woolly hats. Helmets are not obligatory so are seldom worn. One innovation is the use of umbrellas. At one stage during my journey there was rain, and I was amazed to notice that the motorbikes had umbrellas. These slot into a hollow pipe welded on to the motorbike in front of the rider. They are designed in such a way that they cover not only the rider but also any passengers seated behind.

Returning to our hunt for the elusive *matatu*, we seemed to have found termini for *matatus* departing to every town in Kenya except Nyahururu. Eventually, Father Joya was certain we were homing in on the correct location, so while travelling in a very busy street, he suddenly stopped and decided to ask a policeman for assistance. We had missed the turning, which was approximately fifty meters behind us. Turning round in the road was impossible, so unperturbed, the policeman walked behind our vehicle and directed the traffic around us while we reversed the required distance. I was dumbfounded. I could not imagine a policeman doing likewise in London!

Once the terminus had been located, Father Joya made the necessary arrangements for my journey north. He ensured that I was seated in the front of the vehicle. I had no desire to experience the very cramped accommodation in the rear. I said my goodbye to Father Joya. We had not spent long together, but he had told me much about the current situation in Kenya. He is a very knowledgeable but humble man.

Apart from the fact that the driver of my *matatu* seemed to spend most of the time on his mobile phone, the journey to Nyahururu was accomplished with the minimum of fuss.

Jacob, the headmaster of Loiyangalani Primary School, was there to meet me. I had met him previously when he was the headmaster of the El Molo Primary School. We stayed in a hotel where hot water for the shower appeared to be a luxury not available in my room. I was pleased to find Weetabix available for breakfast, but when I doused it with milk from a thermos, I discovered that the milk was hot, so the Weetabix disintegrated into a rather unpleasant mush before I could enjoy it.

The following day we travelled to Maralal in a vehicle belonging to a friend of Jacob's, so a more comfortable journey than that of the previous day. Benedict, who was to be my chaperone for the remainder of my visit, met us there. I have previously mentioned that he is the owner of the Palm Shade Camp where I was to reside in Loiyangalani. Not only was I to be most grateful for him giving up his time to ensure that I could visit all the destinations on my itinerary, but we managed to travel a vast distance, at times on atrocious roads, without having a single puncture. This says a great deal about his driving and the condition of his vehicle.

We set off for Loiyangalani the following day. I had requested this route to Loiyangalani as it was the one that I had used in my initial visits. However, the state of the road over the escarpment north of Maralal was such that it was not the most favoured route at that particular time. The scenery is very picturesque with fabulous views, but the road had deteriorated considerably in recent years. Benedict had to negotiate rocks and potholes that I felt certain would destroy his tyres. Initially, we had to contend with dust, but after an unexpected shower of rain, the surface of the road became slippery. Descending from the escarpment, we travelled into the 'Valley of Tears' as it had been named by the Consolata Fathers, due to the fact that in the early days they were heading into the unknown and often to trials beyond their expectations. At this stage, the desert commences; although not sandy, it is very arid, punctuated by thorn bushes and acacia trees.

We were relieved to reach Baragoi, where we could partake of a late lunch. We selected a café that advertised "fish and chips". I was a little surprised when my companions ordered stew in preference, as I thought it sounded delightful. What could possibly go wrong with fish and chips? When the meal arrived, the chips were as anticipated. The fish was a complete tilapia measuring about twenty-five centimetres from nose to tail. Yes, the head, tail and the fins, complete with spikes, were still attached with no sign of any batter. It had been cleaned, scaled and roasted over a fire. I was expected to consume it in its entirety. I did persuade the proprietor to remove the head, tail and fins, but by that time, not a lot remained. My "fish and chips" had turned into "chips and very little fish"!

The road from Baragoi to South Horr, despite being desert, is very picturesque, as there the terrain is punctuated by hills or small mountains of different shapes and sizes, sometimes standing alone but also constituting two mountain ranges that converge. South Horr is in a valley between the two and experiences a climate unique to the area, so much so that tropical fruit are grown in the locality. There was a welcome splash of colour as local rain had induced many of the plants to flower.

Although both Maralal and Baragoi had grown considerably since my previous visits, South Horr had expanded very little, possibly due to its isolation. Soon after leaving South Horr, the light began to fade. Consequently, my first visit to the massive wind farm of three hundred and sixty-five wind turbines was restricted in that I could only observe the one or two turbines that had been situated close to the road. The ones that I could see were all stationary, which surprised Benedict. It appeared that perhaps none of the turbines were actually in action, a fact that was to be confirmed with a subsequent visit in daylight. This remained puzzling until my return journey south, when we discovered it was not due to the fact that it was the Christmas break!

The next surprise was the level of Lake Turkana. Again, I could not see a great deal, as it was dark. As I have previously mentioned, the lake had risen significantly in the past two years, possibly as the result of a geological incident that had released underground reserves of water, so much so that the road that had been constructed was now under water in one place, rendering it impassable and necessitating a rocky diversion.

It had been a journey full of surprises, and I was glad to reach my destination for a late supper, after which I retired to my room. Mosquito nets had become mandatory at each of the venues where I stayed, so no battles with mosquitoes! It was, however, extremely warm, so sleep was not easy.

The following morning, after breakfast, I met up with Jacob at the primary school. He had managed to persuade a significant number of his students to attend the school despite the fact that the term had actually finished at the end of the previous week. I think the promise of breakfast to all attendees had been used as an incentive. Groups of the students then performed dances and sang songs as a means of expressing their thanks to me for what I had achieved on their behalf. Although, at the time, I did not understand precisely what they were chanting, I did hear my name mentioned several times, and the gesture was greatly appreciated. The students clearly enjoyed the opportunity not only to sing and dance but also to wear their colourful traditional dress.

Once the dancing had ceased, I suggested to Jacob that the students might like to play 'jockeys and horses'[16]. The game was played with no less enthusiasm and chaos than the previous time. Fortunately, one of the teachers was on hand to restore some semblance of order once a comprehension of the rules had been at least partially understood. Determination to succeed was again very much in evidence, with the same tendency to employ shortcuts if the participants thought they could evade detection! I was more than slightly alarmed when a small girl inadvertently wandered into the path of the stampede as they raced around the outside of the circle, only to be completely flattened and ignored until the participants had regained their positions. Covered from head to toe in dust, and obviously bewildered and upset by her experience, she was rescued by a bystander, then brushed down and permitted to resume whatever she had been doing with a minimum of fuss. The participants in the game had been totally oblivious to her plight and had carried on as if she had not been there. Fortunately, no harm was done, but it provided evidence of a totally different mindset when dealing with children in Kenya.

I returned to Palm Shade Camp for my lunch, after which I had a visit from two of the young men, Daniel and Peter, both of whom had been sponsored through the Loiyangalani Trust, but neither by me directly. They were about to commence teaching at Loiyangalani Primary School, which would be the start of careers that should lead to a certain future. Both went to great lengths to thank me for all that I had done. They had both appreciated that it was I who had started the Trust and without my initial vision and determination, their sponsorship would not have happened. It is for moments like this that one strives to do what one can to offer these people the chance for a better future. I was very moved by their words of appreciation.

The following day, Benedict took Daniel, Peter and Damiano, the latter being one of the young men that I sponsor and whose story appears in the following chapter, to two sets of springs, both of which are situated a few miles inland from Loiyangalani. I had requested a visit to both,

[16] See page 103.

because the very first expedition to Lake Turkana had visited them in order to replenish their water supplies. The first was Ngobolong. This is a true oasis in the middle of nowhere. It had not been devastated by goats, and consequently there were copious amounts of green grass, something I had never seen in the area previously and something that clearly surprised my companions. I was informed that in times of plentiful rain, the water flowed directly into the lake, hence the presence of mudfish in its ponds. I did wonder about the sense of relief that must have been experienced by that first expedition upon finding these springs.

From there, Benedict drove us to the second oasis, Laredapach. This was less spectacular, as the area had been devastated by a recent fire and the goats had found the water. On our return journey, Benedict pointed out an area upon which was scattered a large number of rocks below which the soil was apparently very fertile. The removal of the rocks would constitute a formidable task and the location is some way from Loiyangalani, but who knows, one day circumstances may be such that some enterprising organisation may decide to exploit the situation. Cities have sprung up in inhospitable deserts, so why not crops growing in an area strewn with rocks of varying sizes?

Our next destination was the El Molo village that remained attached to the mainland. A boat trip to one of the islands, Bird Island, that had been designated as a nature reserve, had been planned. We arrived in the village to find that preparations were underway. At this stage, having not ventured far on to the lake previously, I had no idea as to the precise whereabouts of our destination or the conditions that we might encounter on the lake. There was an island nearby. Perhaps we were going there – but no, as it turned out. The island that we were destined to visit was some considerable distance from the embarkation point. Had I known the conditions that the lake was preparing to throw at us, I think I might well have decided to remain on *terra firma*! The boat was quite narrow, being about a metre wide as its widest and approximately five metres in length. Stability was not a key feature!

We were presented with lifejackets, which had become mandatory since my previous visit. I was impressed with this regulation, but not quite so impressed by the items we were actually asked to wear. Yes, they were orange and resembled some sort of buoyancy aid, but any 'buoyancy' material appeared to have long since disappeared. Yes, we would probably have been very visible should we have had the misfortune to have been ejected into the lake, but it was likely that the lifejackets could well have been more of a hindrance than a help in our ability to either swim or stay afloat. Nevertheless, we donned them and climbed into the boat. I was seated on the middle fibreglass thwart with one of the lads on either side. It was not long before I had developed a 'numb bum', but as it turned out, this was to be the least of my worries!

We had travelled scarcely two hundred metres when the motor stalled. Given that we had no oars, in fact no secondary means of propulsion, this was a cause for concern. Being relatively close to land, I surmised that, if necessary, we could float sedately towards the shore or gesticulate frantically in the hope that someone might recognise our plight and respond accordingly. We were assured that the problem could be rectified, and sure enough it was, but it was not long before the engine spluttered and stalled again. By this time, we were exposed to all that the lake could throw at us, with a swell bordering on a metre in height and waves being encouraged by a very persistent wind of significant strength. I felt a little like Jesus' disciples on the Sea of Galilee when the storm hit. Unfortunately, there was no Jesus asleep in the stern to calm the sea! Luckily, the problem was addressed for a second time and progress was resumed. Given that the motor was to stall on two more occasions before we reached our destination, the journey was not the most pleasant that I had ever undertaken!

We reached the island that had been named Bird Island. It was not long before I discovered how it had acquired its name. It was a haven for nesting birds. Well, it was until we arrived! Eggs had been laid and the avian residents were far from happy with our presence on the island, dive-bombing us to do all they could to persuade us to make a hasty departure. We did eventually oblige. I believe that our disturbance was minimal, and we did see a variety of species including their eggs, so it was a very interesting visit.

I had anticipated the return journey to be easier than the outward one. The motor appeared to have decided to behave and the wind which had been in our faces had subsided. We had scarcely departed, however, when the wind decided to change direction so that it was not only blowing in our faces but was also rapidly gaining in velocity. It was now an offshore breeze threatening to blow us into the middle of the lake should we have any mechanical problems. It was, in fact, considerably more than a breeze, whipping up white horses on the waves. Having stalled once again, I was beginning to wonder where our journey might terminate. There were no radios or lifeboats. Daniel did not help by recalling a time that he had been forced to spend the whole night on the lake due to a breakdown. Morning had seen him and his companions arrive on the opposite side of the lake. Once the latest breakdown was fixed, our boatsman decided that he would 'go for it'. Regardless of the size of the waves into which we were plunging, and oblivious to the volume of water that was showering his passengers, he proceeded at great speed. It was not long before we were drenched. The lads were also frozen, as they were not used to the conditions.

I think we were unanimous in our gratitude when we did eventually reach the point from which we had originally departed. Even Benedict, who had faced many a danger in his life, told me that he had been very worried. In retrospect, we probably should have had more faith. The two boatmen appear not to have been worried or had any concerns regarding the very temperamental nature of the motor. If they had, they had been very clever at concealing it. Hopefully, if they had had any concerns, we would have aborted the trip at the first sign of an insurmountable problem.

We returned to Palm Shade Camp after a brief halt to have our picnic lunch. Although the sun had ensured that the drying process had commenced, it was good to be able to change into dry clothes.

Benedict then took us to the third of the oases, Mowokiteng Springs. They were closer to Loiyangalani than the other two, so the three lads and I decided to walk back. The oasis was not dissimilar from the first one we had visited earlier in the day. There were copious amounts of green grass and fish in the various ponds. The three sets of springs are obviously fed from the huge reservoir of water that appears to exist under Mount Kulal. It would be interesting to subject the area to a thorough survey to ascertain the extent of this water basin. It was a pleasant walk, following what in rainier times was a river course that would flow into the lake.

The following day was to be spent ascending Mount Kulal. This was not to be as difficult as it may sound. Mount Kulal is actually a lengthy ridge, so attaining the summit is a very gradual climb. Our guide who was residing in Loiyangalani had asked us to ensure that we were ready to leave Palm Shade Camp at 5 am. As I had had to surface shortly after 4 am, I was not that pleased when there was still no sign of him at 5.30 am. Peter and Daniel had decided to accompany me and had arrived on time. I am uncertain whether it was the early start or the length of the walk that had persuaded Damiano not to participate in this particular expedition!

Benedict knew where the guide was staying and so we drove to the hut. The guide was roused and suitably admonished. It was not the best start to what was supposed to be a reasonably long day. As we drove through the wind farm, Benedict's suspicions were confirmed. Not a single turbine was in operation. They stood as silent sentinels over the vast plain.

The final section of the road to Gatab Village, where our expedition was to commence, was atrocious. It had deteriorated markedly since my previous visit. I was unhappy that Benedict had to subject his vehicle to such appalling conditions yet again on my behalf. The fact that there was a light drizzle and visibility was poor, due to the mist swirling round the mountain, did not help.

We disembarked in preparation for the expedition. Both Peter and Daniel had decided that an extra layer of clothing was needed due to the temperature, but for me it was a welcome relief from the heat of Loiyangalani. Benedict remained with the vehicle, as there was a chance that he might have to meet us elsewhere after our descent from the mountain.

Conditions were ideal for me. Despite the fact that the land around Mount Kulal is desert and subject to extreme heat, the mountain complex is of considerable size and attracts rain when the neighbouring land attracts none. Each day whilst in Loiyangalani, I was to observe the mountain complex shrouded in cloud. As it happened, we had selected the day of least rain on which to make the ascent. Views, for the most part, were to be obscured by the mist, but that was normal for the time of year. The mountain complex comprises various gorges and ridges, the highest of which leads to the summit. It was to take us three hours walking from the village to reach the top. The guide did cut me a couple of two-metre walking poles. They were actually very useful, as I have become accustomed to using walking poles in the United Kingdom.

The ascent was notable for two incidents.

At one point, our guide casually pointed to the tracks of a leopard that had obviously used the path the previous evening. We were assured that it was most unlikely that the leopard would be observing us from the foliage of a nearby tree, which was a relief!

I was then amazed a little further along the path to observe none other than Malvolio from Shakespeare's *Twelfth Night*, he of the "yellow

139

stockings" fame, walking towards us. I know that the Kenyans enjoy bright colours, but these knee-length socks were almost dazzling in their appearance. The yellow was exceedingly bright! As it happened, the encounter was very useful; the conveyor of the yellow socks had been prevented from exiting the mountain complex by the gorge that we were to use due to excessive rain. Apparently, there was no way through, and he had been forced to turn back. This saved us a vain attempt.

Reaching the summit was an anticlimax. We were assembled on a particular piece of ground that looked no different from its surroundings when the guide announced that we were indeed standing on the summit. It is the only mountain that I have ever ascended where there has been no obvious peak. The ridge was covered with vegetation, which did not help.

We did a short detour, which involved descending via an extremely muddy path to what was supposed to be a scenic viewpoint. The path was considerably longer and steeper than anticipated, so there was a good deal of slipping and sliding. I am sure the viewpoint was worth the detour, but the prevalence of the mist ensured that we were compelled to use our imagination to ascertain the nature of the view.

We returned to the summit using the same path, which caused us yet more slipping and sliding. Once there, we consumed our picnic lunch. It was a little disconcerting to observe the guide using a machete to slice the mangos. Thankfully, this nasty-looking implement was being used for friendly rather than hostile purposes! I had once been informed that the only logical place to eat a mango is in the bath, as mangos are not the easiest fruit to consume without making a considerable mess.

The summit is approximately two thousand three hundred metres in height. We had actually completed a climb of about fifteen hundred metres from the village. I realised that I had never actually attained this height previously. It was a pity that the summit had not been slightly more significant in order to mark this achievement!

The descent was straightforward. The mist cleared in places, so we were treated to some memorable views. We used a different path near the village so that we could experience the view towards Loiyangalani and the lake. Upon our return, Benedict was waiting patiently. It was not long before his vehicle was again negotiating the collection of rocks and potholes that supposedly constituted a road.

The following day, we were treated to a second boat trip, as I had requested a visit to South Island, the largest of the three islands in the lake. Benedict and I were accompanied by Peter, Daniel and Damiano.

Benedict assured me that we would be using a boat of superior construction to the one that we had used two days ago. It was owned by the fisheries department and had two large outboard motors – still no oars! The life jackets were very similar to those we had used previously.

The lake was still determined to throw what it could at us, presenting us with sizeable waves, but the boat coped admirably, and we soon reached our destination. As we were approaching the beach where we were to disembark, we were treated to a close-up view of a Nile crocodile. These crocodiles are man-eaters and have been known to have done just that. On one of the early expeditions, one of the leaders had watched helplessly as one of his guides had been taken by one of these beasts. Nowadays, they tend to be wary of humans and generally take to the water long before they are approached; No *Jaws* scenarios with crocodiles endeavouring to take large chunks out of visiting craft. It appears that this was a female who had been disturbed while laying eggs, hence her reluctance to leave the beach.

This was the island where two British explorers had disappeared during an early expedition, as described in chapter 2. The inhabitants of the island decided that being bombed by the British was more than a minor inconvenience, and so they had vacated the island hastily. They did leave behind a substantial number of goats, the descendants of which could be seen at least fifty years later still grazing on the island. It is thought they were gradually exterminated by hungry fishermen visiting the island illegally. The waters round the island are protected, so all fishing is illegal. We were to notice one or two groups of fishermen as we circumnavigated the island. Most of these, upon sighting our boat and evidently fearing that we were rangers from the National Park set upon arresting them and confiscating their equipment, made a hasty dash for the interior of the island. Apparently, they are fairly adept at evading the authorities and have hiding places in the nether regions of the island.

It is actually interesting to reflect on how the tribesman and their goats reached the island in the first place. There are two theories.

It is thought that at one time it may have been possible to wade across from the western side of the lake to South Island, as the lake is not that deep in this section; although it is a lot deeper now, especially after the recent increase in depth! I have seen pictures of Lake Naivasha, one of the other lakes further south but part of the Rift Valley system of lakes, completely dry as a result of a series of droughts at the beginning of the twentieth century. Perhaps there was a time under similar circumstances when it would have been possible to walk or wade across from the mainland to the island.

The second theory is that the El Molo tribesmen constructed rafts which they then used to transport themselves and their goats across to the island. If they did, they certainly must have chosen a day when the lake was considerably more docile than it was for either of our days out! It has also been suggested that the goats may have been forced to swim across to the island, possibly tied together in a convoy behind one of the rafts. The mind boggles! Goats are not renowned for their swimming ability, so quite how they would have been induced into the water and then persuaded to embark on what to them would have been a very hazardous journey, I do not know. Quite how they would have survived is a mystery, especially with the odd hungry crocodile lurking in the shallows!

Having landed on the island, we set off to visit the crater for which the island is famous. There has been speculation that the crater is the result of one of the bombs that were dropped. This is unlikely as it is extremely deep but with a comparatively small entrance. The lads endeavoured to ascertain its depth by throwing in small rocks and listening for them to hit the bottom, but they were unable to make any reasonable estimations. They simply concluded that it was deep!

Returning to the boat we circumnavigated the island, disembarking on one more occasion to walk along the airstrip. Apparently, South Island is a popular destination for some of the wealthier residents of Nairobi, who charter a plane and spend the night on the island. Hopefully not too near the crocodiles!

Eventually, the circumnavigation of the island was complete and it was time to head back. I was preparing for a leisurely passage, as there was quite a swell into which we seemed destined to be heading. Anxiety levels were increasing! Our skipper must have been feeling as hungry as I was, because he had other ideas. He opened the throttle and we headed back at considerable speed, bouncing over waves, much to my alarm. Again, the skipper appeared to understand the capabilities of his boat, and so we arrived at our destination without any mishaps.

We returned to Palm Shade Camp for lunch and then a quiet afternoon.

The following day was Christmas Day. How unlike any previous Christmas Day did this particular one turn out to be! I am certain that the locals understood the significance of the day because the majority of them are Catholics. However, apart from attendance at Mass, for most it was no different from any other day. There was no exchange of presents and certainly no special meal with copious amounts of eating and drinking!

After breakfast, I set off to the church to attend Mass. The service lasted three hours, which was unexpected, to say the least. It was prolonged by a dual baptism, but even more so by an unintentional delay. Before commencing the baptism, the priest discovered that he had forgotten to bring the order of service for a baptism, which necessitated a return to his quarters to locate the missing book. Again, I noted the behaviour of the children. Perhaps their way of life is such that they are content to remain inactive for lengthy periods of time. Children in the UK appear to have a constant need to be entertained and do not possess the willpower or patience to remain inactive for any significant period of time unless staring at handheld devices of some description!

Upon leaving the church, I was approached by a lady whom I did not recognise. She introduced herself as the mother of a child that I had assisted in 2005. I described in chapter 4 how I paid for a young boy to have an urgent operation and how the mother and son had accompanied me as far as Maralal. Until this moment, I had had no idea as to the outcome of the operation. For various reasons, she had been waiting seventeen years to say thank you. Later, she brought her son to see me at Palm Shade Camp so that he too could express his thanks. It would appear that the operation may well have saved his life, seemingly to have been more urgent than I had appreciated at the time. It is at times like this that one realises the opportunities that arise in which one can make significant differences, for a comparatively small amount of money, to the lives of those who are absolutely desperate. This was a most unexpected Christmas present!

Benedict and Jacob, together with their wives, joined me for Christmas lunch at Palm Shade Camp. Their company was greatly appreciated, with the meal being very similar to that which I enjoyed on the other days that I was at the camp; no special feast but it did include my customary bottle of beer.

After the meal, I was joined by Peter, Daniel and Damiano as we had a mission. Earlier I mentioned that while in Nairobi, I had purchased a dozen small rockets, which I had planned to set off on the evening of Christmas Day. We had several problems to overcome to ensure that the operation was to be a success. It was decided that we should inform the local police as to our intentions, in case they thought that something untoward was happening. A police raid in the midst of the celebrations would have been most embarrassing.

Initially, we had to assemble a device from which to launch the rockets. Milk bottles were non-existent, beer bottles too tall and cool drink bottles too unstable. We managed to borrow a large rusty can that had certainly seen better days but was an important possession for someone. One of the young men chanced upon a piece of metal pipe. Some of the stony soil was placed in the tin around the piece of pipe so that it was stabilised. The next task was to find somewhere from which to launch the rockets. Given that there was an incessant gale, we needed a location that was sheltered. A family with a stone dwelling kindly gave us permission to use their premises. The final task was to provide a means of igniting the rockets. Matches were conspicuous by their absence. It was decided to light a fire in the cookhouse belonging to the family whose dwelling we were using. The rockets could be ignited using a 'taper' from the burning sticks.

Loiyangalani had never before been the venue for any type of firework display, so as word spread that something unique was about to take place, the audience grew in anticipation. I remained a little apprehensive that a rogue rocket might misfire and land on the roof of one of the many dwellings in the area, most of which were constructed of highly combustible material, in which case the firework display would have been accompanied by a substantial bonfire reminiscent of Guy Fawkes night in the United Kingdom. As it turned out, I need not have worried.

There was one light-hearted moment while we were waiting for darkness to fall. Four youngsters were sitting of an improvised 'bench' made from a plank of wood. I am not quite certain why, but the plank suddenly upended itself, causing the four youngsters to fall over backwards so that four sets of feet and little else were all that was visible. It was reminiscent of one of the scenes from a comedy movie from the early days of cinema. Fortunately, there were no injuries but copious amounts of laughter.

After a few renditions of 'We wish you a Merry Christmas', it was decided that there was sufficient darkness to commence the launching of the rockets. Quite what the youngsters expected, I have no idea. The lad charged with lighting each rocket once it had been inserted in the pipe performed his task admirably. One by one, each rocket ascended into the sky, bursting into colour, to gasps of amazement from the children. It was a sight to behold. Once the stash of rockets had become exhausted, I provided some sparklers for the spectators. These were enjoyed by those who managed to procure one, but almost resulted in civil war amongst the spectators. Luckily, the supply was exhausted before there was serious injury. This was perhaps not the best of my ideas. I was humbled yet again to realise how things we often take for granted in this country can bring so much joy to those who have nothing. On the following day, it was to become apparent that virtually every soul in Loiyangalani had either observed or heard about the fireworks of the previous evening.

The following day, Benedict drove me and four of the lads north to the village of Moite. The distance to the village was approximately one hundred kilometres. This settlement had been very sparse when last visited with Father Joya, so I was keen to see how much it had grown. An alternative road had been constructed, so we proceeded by this inland route, which was less scenic than the original road running alongside the lake. Benedict continued to amaze me. I knew he had been in the area for a considerable amount of time, but he seemed to know everyone. We encountered several people wandering along the road; Benedict knew every one of them, greeting them as fond friends.

Once in Moite, I could appreciate that, like the other villages in the area, it had grown considerably. We visited two of the students who were being sponsored by the Loiyangalani Trust. The village now had its own primary school, but in the past the children from the village had had to attend the Loiyangalani Primary School.

We decided to return via the old road. It continued to be used by those wishing to visit the small communities who had settled along the shore of the lake. The journey was lengthier than the outward one, but more interesting. Fortunately, the recent increase in the water level of the lake had not intruded upon the road, although it was quite close in several places.

We did pass one or two of the small settlements residing at the edge of the lake. I was moved to contemplate their way of life. They build their huts. They possess a few goats. They fish, selling a few that are surplus to requirements in order to supplement their resources. They marry and have children. The cycle is maintained in much the same way as it has been for generations. They are safer than they used to be, as raiding from other tribes has ceased. They appear to be content. They have no bills to pay. They are unlikely to be affected by any diseases, such as Coronavirus. We, from the UK, are trying to present them with opportunities to 'better' the lives of their children through education. Surely, it could be argued that they are happy as they are. Why do they need to change? Obviously, everything is relative, but there are many people living in the United Kingdom who do have the opportunity to be educated and yet it has done little for them; their families struggle to make ends meet with prices continuing to rise so that income is outpaced by expenditure. Yes, they have access to free healthcare and other benefits, but are they happier than these families living on the edge of the lake? Is waking up in a small flat on a rainy day in London with financial worries really preferable to waking up in a hut on the edge of the lake with glorious sunshine, fantastic views and no monetary concerns? Food for thought?

Before reaching Loiyangalani, we stopped at Mount Porr. This is nothing like Mount Kulal in height, but it is a conical landmark with outstanding views of the surrounding country and the lake. It is visible from Loiyangalani and has always been a landmark that I have wished to climb. It has very steep rocky slopes interspersed with annoying thorn bushes, each one of which seemed to have positioned itself on the route that I had decided to use to ascend the mountain. After a significant amount of huffing and puffing, with a few stops to rehydrate, I did reach the summit to join the four lads who had skipped up the mountain like mountain goats, but the climb had been more difficult than I had anticipated due to the heat. It brought back memories of another expedition I had undertaken on a previous visit! The views were amazing, making the climb most worthwhile. The descent was interesting, as most of the rocks upon which I decided to perch myself were decidedly unstable! We did locate a sandy section, which was descended with ease. After waiting patiently, Benedict then drove us back to Palm Shade Camp. We enjoyed another spectacular sunset on the way.

The final day was spent 'tying up loose ends'. I was invited to plant two trees in the grounds of Loiyangalani Primary School. I had planted a tree on a previous visit, but it appears not to have survived, so hopefully at least one of these two may fare slightly better!

We had a very interesting supper on the final day. I think the lads realised that it could be a while before they had the opportunity to consume copious amounts of food, so they took full advantage of the generous spread provided by Benedict's staff, with plates overflowing with the various items. Jacob then gave us a very interesting insight into various aspects of Kenyan history regarding the Mau Mau[17] and his feelings about colonialism[18]. As I was to be departing early on the following day, we said our goodbyes.

My journey south was to span two days. Benedict was my chauffeur for most of it. Our first stop was to be the wind farm, and it was not long before we were informed as to the reason for the stationary nature of the turbines. The electricity travels south to Naivasha via a series of pylons, some of which we had observed on the journey to Loiyangalani. Due to the fact that this line had been required to travel in as straight a line as possible, some of the pylons had been erected in locations that are not only remote but often precarious in nature. As a consequence, security arrangements for the protection of the line are very limited and in places non-existent. We were informed that the line to Naivasha had been cut, with the copper wire being removed and probably exchanged for a significant sum of money. How one actually severs a cable through which is flowing vast amounts of electricity without becoming 'fried', I have no idea. It did strike me as bizarre that a multi-million-pound project could be brought to a standstill by a simple act of vandalism. Of course, the power line is extremely vulnerable, but surely consideration should have been given to what one must assume should have been a very obvious weakness in the project so that this scenario could have been avoided?

Isiolo was our initial destination, which we reached as it was getting dark. I had made two interesting observations regarding road travel in Kenya.

There are police checkpoints in the most unexpected locations. For most drivers, it is a matter of waving to a friendly policeman, who will then remove whatever obstacle has been placed across the road, often a particularly gruesome-looking tyre shredder. On the road to Isiolo, we were actually stopped at a major checkpoint, and I was required to present my passport to the police. Quite who they thought I might be, I have no idea. Benedict informed me that they were looking for suspicious vehicles that might contain terrorists. I am uncertain as to the number of terrorists who would brazenly drive down a main road in broad daylight and calmy present themselves to a police checkpoint! At least the police are seen as being proactive in the constant battle against terrorism.

[17] See page 162.
[18] See page 168.

There are very few speed-limit signs in Kenya, particularly outside Nairobi. There is, however, an extremely efficient deterrent for those who would wish to speed through towns and villages. A series of enormous speed humps have been constructed on the approach to and within each location where there is some form of habitation. I think that if one were to attempt to drive over one of these at anything more than a walking pace, driver and passengers would be propelled into the air and the vehicle would suffer extensive damage. These humps were constructed in such a way that they stretched beyond the edges of the road, so thoughts of circumnavigation were pointless; simple but effective means of ensuring speed limits are adhered to.

We spent the night in a local hotel. These hotels would probably not pass any health and safety checks in the United Kingdom, but the staff are always very friendly and eager to please. It is interesting what one takes for granted in hotels. Each hotel required the climbing of concrete steps to reach one's assigned room. I could not understand why I would stumble ascending these steps. It was certainly not due to the excessive imbibing of alcohol! It was only upon having tripped for the umpteenth time that I decided to investigate. In the United Kingdom, steps in any given set of stairs would usually be identical, but in Kenya they are not. The height of each step can actually vary by at least a centimetre, sufficient to cause the unwary user to stumble. It would appear that our minds have been programmed to assume that the steps in any given staircase will be of identical height, so one ascends or descends without the need to concentrate. The mounting of these steps in the Kenyan hotels requires attention to the height of the individual steps if one is not to make a complete fool of oneself.

The following day, Benedict took me to Nanyuki, where we parted company. He had been a brilliant host and chauffer. I did appreciate all he had done to ensure that I was well looked after. He had ensured that I had visited all the venues that I had requested at the outset.

My flight from Nanyuki to Nairobi had been negotiated by Father Joya. As he had departed to be with his family, he had kindly arranged for one of the other Consolata Fathers, Father Denis, to collect me from the airport. Although I knew what time the flight departed, there seemed to be some confusion over its time of arrival in Nairobi. It was a thirty-minute direct flight but seemed to arrive at its destination forty-five minutes earlier than expected, although I was unaware of the scheduled arrival time when I boarded the plane. It was suggested that originally it had probably been scheduled to fly via another regional airport to offload and collect passengers. Possibly due to lack of demand, the flight had headed straight to Nairobi. Taking off from Nanyuki had not been without its moments of apprehension. It had been raining. The runway was muddy, and the plane had to taxi through the mud and puddles in order to become airborne. I had visions of performing a slalom along the runway. As it happened, the pilot appeared very accustomed to the conditions and performed a faultless take-off.

Once I had arrived at my destination, confusion reigned! There was no sign of Father Denis! I had no contact number, so was uncertain what to do. In fact, the only contact I could make was with Jacob in Loiyangalani, who tried unsuccessfully to contact him. Being unsure of my planned time of arrival in Nairobi, I waited for a while and then decided to take a taxi to the Consolata Seminary. This was not that straightforward, as the taxi drivers seemed to have little idea as to its location. I told them it was in Langata Road, but I might as well have said it was somewhere on the M6, such was the length of Langata Road! One taxi driver decided he could find it, so having eventually located his keys which he had managed to mislay, we did eventually depart. It would appear that as we were leaving the airport, Father Denis was probably arriving. Unwisely, he was to leave his vehicle unattended for a few moments in an effort to locate me, only to find on his return that it had been clamped! Apparently, 'clampers' operate very swiftly in the area, eager to make as much money as possible! Poor Father Denis was compelled to part with an exorbitant sum of money in order to be reunited with his car. All in all, the experience had cost both of us more money that had been intended with the original set of plans.

Eventually, Father Denis and I were united at the Consolata Seminary, with my taxi driver having found the destination after conversations with various helpful souls in the area. After lunch, Father Denis took me to finalise a few pressing needs, one of which was the need to have the obligatory Coronavirus test so that I could fly to the United Kingdom the following day. He was certain there was plenty of time to have the test and receive the result.

We duly arrived at a testing centre. While completing the required paperwork, I informed the clerk at the desk that I needed the result by 2 pm the following day, as I had to be at the airport at that time. I was informed that this would be impossible. The result would not be available until 3 pm. I pointed out that this would be too late to satisfy immigration

149

at the airport. Apparently, nothing could be done! Most unhelpful! Fortunately, Father Denis understood the situation immediately. There were three administrators involved with the testing process. He took one of them aside, and it soon became apparent that a bribe would resolve the situation. Of course, this had to be arranged discretely, as it was completely illegal. Bank account details were exchanged and money transferred. The test results were with me by 10 am the following morning!

This is an aspect of Kenyan life that is so despicable. As I have mentioned elsewhere, I am aware that 'palms' are still 'greased' in the United Kingdom in order that situations can be resolved favourably for certain parties, but it is not quite so blatantly obvious. Bribing remains commonplace in Kenya. Both Father Joya and Jacob had informed me that it is an aspect of life in Kenya of which they are ashamed. Throughout my visit, I had always found the locals so keen to help, and so it was a disappointment to discover a group who wished to take advantage of me.

This trip to Loiyangalani had probably been the best of all the trips that I had made. It had been good to renew old acquaintances and make new friends. I had achieved all that I had set out to achieve and more. I had visited places that I had never previously visited, experiencing at different times copious amounts of both joy and anxiety! It served to reignite my enthusiasm to assist the people of Loiyangalani in as many ways as possible.

CHAPTER TEN

Raphael and Damiano

I asked Raphael and Damiano to write a short description of their lives thus far. I have decided to reproduce them exactly as they have been written, amending punctuation and spelling where necessary.[19] It is worth remembering that both entered primary school without being able to speak a word of English.

There are similarities in the accounts, but also elements that are unique to each. Hence the decision to use both. It is interesting to understand how they have perceived their lives and what they have considered to have been of importance. I have not omitted the very kind words that they have included about me, as my intervention was a major influence on their lives. The sponsorship has changed the paths down which they would have inevitably been forced without it.

Raphael's Life Experiences and Academic Journey

FAMILY BACKGROUND

I take this chance to thank Almighty God for the gift of life up to this far. I am Raphael Chamah Epeyon – born in a family of eight. My parents are Epeyon Longole and Gabriella Epeyon. In a nutshell, we are three boys and five girls. We live in Loiyangalani, along the south-eastern shores of Lake Turkana, in the former eastern province of Kenya. I lost two siblings – a sister and a brother and later my dad in the year 2010. I was then in Class Seven in Loiyangalani Primary School. My parents were pastoralists, and they didn't know the importance of education. They only believed livestock keeping was the only way to get through

---

[19] Grammar, flow and word choice/usage have not been corrected.

life. My dad was a craftsman, he made nice walking sticks, knives and small stools (called *Ekicholong* in our local Turkana language). He mostly sold them to the visiting tourists at relatively low prices.

We mostly relied on natural herbs for medication, as cost for hospital was a bit high for such a mere person. Meeting the basic needs was a big challenge for our family – just imagine staying all day without food. Many are times we could go a day without breakfast, or lunch and sometimes even without supper.

Mom used to burn charcoal as an alternative source of income. She would sell to at least get some little cash for buying food for the family.

We live in a thatched house made from wooden sticks and doum palm leaves. The materials for building are fetched from far. The hut is covered with palm leaves on the top and mud is spread all round on the sides to protect people inside from the strong winds in the area, and as well as to provide support for the hut. The hut is usually temporal since it can only last for up to six years before it is demolished and a new one is built. Worse thing is, all family members sleep in the same hut until you are grown up. In most cases, no mattresses nor beds. People sleep on animal skins spread on the ground, exposing us to risks of bites from scorpions, spiders and snakes.

Most children at a tender age would go without any clothes nor shoes on until they join school. So did I.

When I was a young boy, my daily routine during holidays was to fetch water and look after our three goats. I would also go for hook and line fishing at the shores of the lake.

Looking after goats was hectic and tiresome experience since I have to take them to a far place to seek pasture and water. Not forgetting that I would go the whole day without food.

I used to play hide and seek with my close friends, particularly at night.

EDUCATION BACKGROUND

In the year 2003, the Kenyan government announced the free primary education program. That is when I enrolled for school at Loiyangalani Primary School. I never attended nursery school. The only available by then was Consolata Nursey School, which was managed by the missionaries, and fees was necessary for every term. So, children from poor backgrounds could not get the opportunity to join.

At Loiyangalani Primary School, the classes were relatively smaller with few desks. Some classes even had none. Pupils in lower classes would sit on mats spread on the floor. At least we would study regardless.

At some point, the school was overpopulated, therefore mounting pressure on the available scarce resources. Space was limited, but we would at least find some space on the floor to sit. I remember, there was a time while I was still in primary school, the Loiyangalani Trust Fund donated chairs and desks for pupils and the school staff.

There was scarcity of books and revision materials in the school and access to them was a challenge. Sometimes the school management is forced to chase pupils home, to come back with full school uniform, money to buy fuel wood or each one to come with a piece of firewood. The moment I don't get fees or uniform, I had no option but to skip classes. The cost for school uniform and firewood was KSH 500 (approx. £3.00) and KSH 100 (approx. £0.60) respectively. Although sometimes I would risk attending classes as it was not allowed for those who do not have school uniform or failed to come with money for fuel wood. By then, the late Mr Bosco Ekal, was the school headteacher and for sure he had a human heart. He admitted pupils from poor backgrounds without school uniform.

When I was in Class Two, one of the Consolata priests provided us with school uniforms which I wore for a couple of years – about six.

I liked playing football. I used to play football as a winger, and my friends had nicknamed me "Solomon Kalou". He was my favourite football idol. He played for Chelsea Football Club. I also loved athletics, particularly long-jump and short races.

The school, Loiyangalani Primary, used to provide lunch for pupils. In days when there was no food in school, many pupils would fail to attend school. When I was in Class Six, I joined boarding basically to access meals and enough time for studies since we could not have consistent meals at home.

I was in Class Six when you brought us apples. And by the way, that was the first time I saw and ate an apple fruit. We were so excited for your kind support.

In 2011, I sat for Kenya Certificate of Primary Education (KCPE) where I performed well and I received admission letter from Kivaywa Boys' High School, a school located in western Kenya. Unfortunately, I could not attend Kivaywa Boys' School as my mom could not raise the money needed for my school fees, fare and upkeep. I planned to rather go back to primary school and repeat the primary school because of the inability to join high school. Since that would be a waste of time and the little resources that were available, my mom had no choice but to sell her three goats to buy me school uniform and shoes. Soon later, I joined Loiyangalani Secondary School without school fees. They'd at some point admit students from poor background without anything – not even money to buy books. Luckily, I was admitted to the school.

In 2012, I heard about your visit to Loiyangalani. Ekori Albert, who's also a Trust beneficiary informed me about you and some of the team members (Loiyangalani Trust) that you had arrived in Loiyangalani. I decided to write a letter requesting for support. Then one afternoon, I heard that you were at the primary school and I decided to sneak out of school and go after you. I believed I will get some help. And thanks, you did so! I studied from form one to form three in the same school (Loiyangalani Secondary) before I transferred to Nyiro Boys' High School, which was about 90 km south of Loiyangalani.

Later, I and my friends from the Trust requested for a move to a better school. Nyiro Boys' High School had a good studying environment as it was situated in at least a cool place than Loiyangalani. I would say, life at Nyiro Boys' High was quite different as compared to the previous school.

Upon arrival at Nyiro Boys' High, I couldn't imagine students were already done with the syllabus up to Form Four, yet we were barely halfway with Form Three work. Worst thing yet, I had chosen to do geography and do away with history, but history was must do subject in Nyiro Boys' High. So, there was no space for doing both. Due to the situation, I had to pick history and government and leave alone geography. I was then instructed by the subject teacher to write full notes for that subject. For sure, I had sleepless nights and sometimes the subject tutor threatens me because I had no idea about that subject. After two terms, we sat for end of term exams and I emerged the best student of history and government. Wow! The subject tutor couldn't believe. He was so happy of me.

I can't also forget there was a time my stomach was bothering me for long. I got admitted at Loiyangalani Consolata missionary dispensary and in good luck you happened to be around, and you offered to pay the hospital bills. I appreciate for that sir! You also paid for my mom's eyes medication. She's so grateful for your kind support.

In the year 2015, I sat for Kenya Certificate of Secondary Education (KCSE) and I attained a mean grade of B- 58 points. After I completed secondary school, it was another great opportunity that I went for computer course at Sagana Technical Training Institute for a couple of three months. I and fellow friends, like Bonke Chechekuna, Augustine Ekale and Adriano Lopir enjoyed the serene environment, exposure and opportunity to learn computer skills. It was then my first time to travel out of Loiyangalani to such a far place. It was really exciting to see lots of different vehicles on the road, access to different meals and fruits, most of which were new to me, and best part each one of us was awarded a certificate upon completion of the computer course.

The grade I had scored in high school was enough to get me to university. I am so happy Anthony Mitchell has always been in the forefront to cater for my varsity education. He has whole heartedly catered for everything! I'm so grateful.

I enrolled for a degree in Bachelor of Science in Fisheries and Aquaculture with Information Technology in September 2016 at Maseno University. Last year, I went for industrial attachment at Kenya Marine and Fisheries Research Institute (KMFRI) Sang'oro Station for three months. Life at the campus has been different from the kind of life I was used to at the village. I'm happy to be in practical, research and real-life world. My dream is to be a scientific researcher in the field of aquaculture and alleviate poverty and malnutrition, enhance employment creation and food security through multidisciplinary and collaborative research in freshwater aquatic systems.

Me being the first child to join school in a family of eight, I have convinced my mom to let others join school, and luckily, I got one brother and two sisters in primary school. The community have realised the importance of education and so far, a good number of children are in school. Sometimes I and fellow Loiyangalani Trust beneficiaries take the initiative to enlighten the community about the importance of education.

I'm so glad to have you in my life.

Thank you for believing in me, for words of encouragement and endless support throughout my academic journey.

Thanks, Loiyangalani Trust for laying the foundation of my education, giving it all it takes.

Thank you again, sir!

Regards,

Raphael Chamah

The Story of Sponsored Child, Damiano

MY ACADEMIC AND SOCIAL LIFE HISTORY

I take this opportunity to thank the Lord for the gift of life, the far He has taken me up to now to narrate my academic and social life experience about my life. I am Damiano Lokai Etelej, born on 2nd February 1998 at Loiyangalani in Nawapa Village, 0.5 km away from Loiyangalani Primary School. I was managed and raised by my affectionate mother, Mary Etelej and father, Etelej Korikel, but unfortunately, we lost him on 29th May 2017 due to health problems. Both my parents came from Loriu Hills as they were based on pastoralism way of life. They later migrated along the shores of Lake Turkana, where they settle at Loiyangalani, Nawapa Village. They were never educated, since at their time education had no value. Girls were used as part of dowry and boys were meant to take care of animals and defend the community. I was born in a family of eight children, six boys and two girls.

I am the fifth born of our family. At the age of five years, I was introduced to take care of the goats and sheeps. It was the main role and culture for boys or men to take care of animals, though they were few in number, about five goats and three sheeps. Drought and famine was a great challenge that we faced, since we depend on animals for meat and milk. My mother also used to burn charcoal to make the end meet in order to satisfy the basic want to all of us. She used to go and seek jobs from well-being families in order to ensure we get something to eat. As times goes, she was able to be employed temporary as a cleaner at Loiyangalani Consolata Sisters Health Centre.

Our home structure was temporary since we developed the pastoralism and nomadism way of life. We used to travel long distance with the animals to look for green pasture for the animals. Due to the hardship and humble background which I grew up with, I was able to endure the harsh and hostile conditions of the environment that we lived to herd the animals we had. Our home was in form of hut; it never required measurement skills and time to make it. A big circle was drawn by use of leg to estimate the number of people that the house would accommodate. The house was made of palm tree leaves, mud, logs of acacia trees, covered with animal skins and manilla paper at the top to prevent rain and hot rays of the sun. We used to spend with our family members at the same house.

I experience the attack of scorpions and snake bite, especially when I was herding the animals, as the land was bushy with a lot of grasses and rocks. It happen one day when I was bitten by a scorpion to get medication was a big problem. There was no hospital or dispensary to access easily; herbs from trees was used to calm the situation. The land was made of rocks. When I was taking care of the animals, rocks were very important. Some were made of V shape which enable to hold water during the rainy seasons, this enable me to satisfy my thirst when I was herding the animals. My father was able to break rocks and to sell to those who were able to build bricks houses. He had masonry skills and ability to make quarry stones for building houses. He never went to school to gain knowledge, but he had that skill to do any kind of work. Sometimes we herd our animals with my friends around Lake Turkana, where we used to go to swim as the animals were grassing.

I was good in composing the traditional songs which we used to sing with my friends to pass time as we herd the animals. We used to grass the livestock nearer to Loiyangalani Primary School. Whereby, I decided one day to go and peep at the window to know what people were doing inside the classrooms. Pupils were taught by a teacher. Children laugh at me since I never had clothes and shoes. I started developing the interest and eager to join them. When I went home, I assemble my mum and dad, to tell them that I wish also to be educated like the other pupils. It became a long discussion whereby it took time for them to decide and come up with the solution to take me to school.

I joined Loiyangalani Primary School. I never attended the nursery school. The only nursery school available was Consolata Nursery, which was private, run and managed by the Consolata Sisters from Italy. In 2003, following the directive from the Government of Kenya and the Ministry of Education, free primary was introduced all over the country to ensure all people had access to education. I was able to join Loiyangalani Primary School in 2006, whereby I started my academic journey. I remember classes were too small for the large enrolment of pupils. To write on the desk was a problem since there was no space even to stretch the hand to write what was taught. There was insufficiency of coursework book to read or to write the exercise given by the teacher.

In 2009 when I was in Class Five, sir, I remember when you came to Loiyangalani, whereby you stay at Loiyangalani Catholic mission. That moment we had our Physical Education nearer to the Church since we had our small field with no goal post. I saw you carrying boxes of apples with a land-cruiser. I decide to run and open the mission gate. I greeted you and surely you told me your name was Anthony. As we were playing, we were told by the teacher to assemble to our normal respective class because we had a visitor. That moment I was the class monitor. We were so cheerful and happy when you entered to our class with a lot of apples. That was the day that I ate an apple and know how it taste. This was how I knew you. Actually, it was a cheerful moment also to us. We sang some nice songs to you. You introduce yourself to us that you are called Anthony Mitchell from United Kingdom (UK), that you wanted to help the needy pupils from humble background, discipline and clever pupils. Your visit made a great impact to our school, whereby you went back to the United Kingdom to seek help from other well-wishers to come up with the Loiyangalani Trust Fund team to ensure the school had better desks for pupils and teachers. In school, I was elected as the school head boy in 2013 when I was in Class Eight. I used to play football as a goalkeeper at our village. Raphael, being my team striker and a winger, Number 7, he use to score many scores for us managing to be the best team against other village team.

I sat my Class Eight exam for the Kenya Certificate of Primary Education in 2013, where I manage to score 300 marks out of 500 marks. We became the most improve school in Northern Kenya in Marsabit County. The school performance attracted many pupil to join our school, hence leading to mass enrolment of pupils to study.

The hard moment was when I completed my Class Eight course; there was lack of fees to join secondary school. Loiyangalani Secondary School was the only school around. I stayed at home for around two months to seek for fees. My mum and dad decided to sell the few goats that we had to enable me to go to school. It really hurts me when some of my colleagues were joining school. My mum and dad got the fee of only one term. I was taken to school without other necessities like school uniform with few books to write on. Three subjects was for only one book.

I stayed in the school for almost one week. The following week, the student break for mid-term holiday. I was happy when I heard that you are coming to Loiyangalani with other Trust Fund friends in 2014. I heard Albert Ekori say that you are around. Good luck, I was among those who got your help. We met at Palm Shades Resort, where we had a long talk with you. We had meal together, discussing also which school we will join with other students benefitting from the Loiyangalani Trust Fund. We also had a walk to our home where you took some pictures. We were taken to Nyiro Boys' High in Samburu County by the late Mr Bosco Ekal. The school was so conducive to study, with well-equipped resources. In 2017, I sat for my Kenya Certificate of Secondary Education where I attained a mean grade of D+ with 31 points. The result was not quite fine as per my capability. During our time, the performance all over the county was deteriorating. The government reduced the entry of grade to join colleges and universities all over the country as per the courses taken by students. I never lose hope towards your help because you were a helping hand.

I joined Mount Kenya University in 2018, taking a course in Certificate in Information Technology in the School of Computing and Informatics. For two years, I had a serene environment in the school. I developed a passion in the field of Information Technology (IT), specialising my dream of becoming computer expert on network design, database developer and system analyst. The course is so advantageous since one can be employed in any field of employment opportunities. Also, Kenya is having a vision on 2030 whereby everything will be digitalised through advanced technology through computerization of work. I had my attachment at Provision General Hospital (PGH) Level 5, in the Department of Information Technology, where I employed my skills gain in school. I did some activities assigned to me during the industrial attachment, e.g. updating of software and hardware, resolution of local area network, computer hardware upgrade, configuration of anti-virus in the computer system and providing matters concerning information communication technology. Life at the campus seems so different from the village. It has taught me to be a self-responsible man and endorsing me to the real practical world. I could not have gone so far, because of your support, sir. May you be blessed. You are a real pioneer to be remember for the good initiative that you took to help people from the Loiyangalani fraternity.

Thank you for trusting and believing in me and for your massive support through my academic journey.

Thank you again.

Yours faithfully,

Damiano Lokai Etelej

These accounts reveal some of the hardships experienced by both young men. Unfortunately, for many, life in the village has not changed. The great hope is that in time, it will do so.

CHAPTER ELEVEN

The Consolata Missionaries

In this chapter, I will give a brief summary about the Consolata Missionaries and the part they played in the history of Loiyangalani and Kenya in general. I include a section on religious beliefs and conclude with the story of Father Joya, who has played a vital part in enabling me to support the community in Loiyangalani.

The Consolata mission was established by Joseph Allamano in Turin in Italy. The official date for their foundation is given as 29th January 1901. It is therefore relatively young when compared with other missions operating in Africa. It is a Catholic organisation named after Our Lady Consolata, which uses the image of the virgin Mary as 'consoled' or 'consoler'.

The initial group of the missionaries arrived in Kenya in 1902, celebrating their first official Mass in Tuthu on 29th June 1902. The first nuns arrived a year later. Not only was the country of Kenya as we know it today in its infancy, but the Consolata Missionaries were very much the 'new boys on the block'. Establishing themselves as a viable organisation was to be no easy task, as there were other missionaries from Christian denominations that were liable to be wary of intruders with little or no experience of missionary work.

The aims of the Consolata mission were not solely to evangelise, although that was a high priority, but to support the local communities through a variety of initiatives. Caring for the sick by establishing dispensaries, educating the young by building schools and generally endeavouring to integrate themselves into the local communities by developing an understanding of the nature and customs of the local tribes in the areas where the missions were to be established were high on the agenda. They also created orphanages for children who, for various reasons, had no family capable of caring for them. The missionaries ensured that as a priority they learnt the local language to facilitate communication. There was a strong desire to work together with the local community. A seminary was soon established so that members of the local tribes could become catechists.

Upon reaching the interior, having arrived on the coast, one of their initial projects was to build a sawmill, perhaps not something one would have thought to have been a priority, but nevertheless parts were summoned from Italy. Unfortunately, the enthusiasm for the project was greater in Italy than in Kenya, where initial local opposition had to be overcome! Being a very young organisation, they had to contend with opposition not only from missionaries from other denominations but also from those of the same denomination. They had to ensure that they were not perceived to be encroaching on the territory of the well-established missions. Although literally 'singing from the same hymn sheet', suffice it to say harmony did not always prevail!

The difficulties concerning the undertaking became more apparent when two of the newly arrived nuns died within a month of each other, succumbing to unknown illnesses.

Missionaries from all denominations were regarded as second-class citizens by the British administration. The situation was compounded further by the fact that the Consolata Missionaries were Italian. Dealing with issues such as racism and elitism did not ensure smooth progress in their endeavours. With the advent of the Second World War, the situation deteriorated further. Being Italian, the unfortunate missionaries were 'on the wrong side', as a consequence of which they were arrested and interned. The idea that these Italian missionaries who had lived and worked in the country for many years should suddenly be perceived as a threat to national security seems to be absurd. Quite why and how they might wish to secrete information out of the country remains a mystery. It was a case of being in the wrong place on the wrong side at the wrong time.

Having suffered the indignity of internment for most of the duration of the Second World War, the missionaries were soon faced with their next challenge. All Christian missionaries were to suffer in some way during the Mau Mau uprising. It is necessary to explain a little about the Mau Mau before proceeding further.

The Mau Mau was predominantly an organisation consisting of members of the Kikuyu tribe. Although the ultimate goal of the Mau Mau was to regain land that had been appropriated by the colonial administration, it has often in the past, and still is, mistakenly claimed that seeking independence was its prime goal.

On my most recent visit, Jacob explained the situation. Given that at least two of the lads sitting round the table were about to commence teaching, it may have been very much for their benefit. Apparently, the Mau Mau feature prominently in history lessons as being the catalyst in the fight for independence. Jacob pointed out that this was incorrect, and propaganda may well play its part in this teaching. Jacob insisted that the Mau Mau had been fighting for the repossession of lands taken from them by the British, and independence would have happened regardless of their activity.

The movement's adherents also sought to ensure that all Christian Kikuyus should renounce their Christian beliefs and take an oath to follow the traditional beliefs of their tribe. This 'persuasion' often involved unbelievable cruelty, and the intervention of the missionaries seemed to 'fan the flames' of resentment. Not only were indigenous catechists murdered for refusing to renounce their faith, but white missionaries, both male and female, suffered the same fate. It was a difficult time not only for the white settlers but also for Christians from all walks of life. Eventually the uprising fizzled out, but not before atrocities had been committed by both sides.

With the establishment of independence, life became less precarious for the missionaries. There remained, however, risks, especially when travelling. In 1965 Father Stallone, having reached Loiyangalani, was murdered by a gang of thirty bandits, known as *shiftas*.[20] Upon my most recent visit to Loiyangalani, I had been able to speak to a survivor of the attack who as a young lad had managed to hide from the bandits when they attacked, but he remembers the event as being especially terrifying.

In 1981 Father Graiff, while travelling between the settlements of Parkati and Tuum, both south of Lake Turkana, was ambushed and killed by local bandits called *Ngoroko*. Although the Consolata Missionaries were generally respected by the local people, travelling in northern Kenya remained a risky undertaking, especially in times of drought when needy individuals considered any traveller to be a worthy target.

---

[20] See page 23.

Especially in the early years, the life of the missionaries arriving from the comparative comforts of Italy must have been very tough. They were convinced of the need to spread Christianity to all parts of the globe and at the same time improve the living conditions of the local communities. I discuss the concept of 'indoctrination' in greater detail in the next section. Regardless as to what one may think regarding the indoctrination of indigenous people, there is no doubt that many lives were saved through the introduction of the dispensaries and the distribution of even basic medicine. As I mention elsewhere, education provided for the most part in the early years by the missionaries assisted in no small way in the eventual push for independence. Whereas today there are charities such as the Loiyangalani Trust that provide additional finance to improve the lives of local communities, when the missionaries arrived, these charities did not exist.

I believe that missionaries like those from the Consolata mission have over the years improved the lives of many Kenyans, most of whom are very grateful for the assistance that has been given.

Before leaving this chapter, it is worth examining the whole idea of missionary zeal and 'indoctrination' that has been the subject of criticism in recent years.

There are those who argue that if one has strong religious beliefs, there should be the opportunity to convey these beliefs so that the recipients can decide for themselves whether or not to adopt these ideas. In theory, it should be a simple matter of choice. Unfortunately, life is not straightforward. Often 'carrots' in the form of food, medicine and education have accompanied the spread of the Christian doctrine. Accompanying a new message or set of beliefs with 'goodies' has often clouded the issue in such a way that the adoption of the new set of beliefs may well have come about for the wrong reasons.

Before dismissing 'indoctrination' or missionary activity as unacceptable interference, it is worth considering the motives behind the intervention. There is no doubt that the missionaries felt inspired or 'called' to missionary work. They believed that they had a message that the Kenyan tribes needed to hear. In addition, they wished to show that accompanying this message was a genuine desire to improve the lives of the communities in which they worked. For my readers who are non-Christians, it is worth a brief explanation as to why these missionaries considered the spread of Christianity to be of such importance. I do not intend to produce a lengthy theological dissertation in an effort to convert my readers to Christianity, but a brief statement might clarify the situation.

Christians believe in some form of positive life after death. According to the teachings of Christ in the Bible, this can only be obtained by surrendering one's life to Christ and following his commands. The teachings also suggest that the consequences of ignoring his teaching are undesirable to say the least! His followers have been asked to spread the 'word' to all corners of the earth. Throughout the ages since the command was first given, many people, convinced as to the genuineness of this message, have devoted their lives to this cause. Starting with his disciples and then continued by various devotees over the intervening centuries, many of his followers have suffered excruciating torture and horrendous deaths because they were utterly convinced as to the veracity of this message.

A trivial comparison could be made with the following scenario: If one was in a position where one was privy to information that a severe hurricane or tsunami was en route to devastate a particular region, one would do one's utmost to ensure that the message reached any in its predicted path in order that they would have time to remove themselves to a location perceived to be safe. If, however, this involved swimming across a crocodile-invested river, risking one's life to warn a group that could not be contacted by any other means, I am not quite so certain that there would be that many volunteers, but there would undoubtedly be some if they believed that lives could be saved! These volunteers would risk their own lives to ensure that the message reached those for whom the situation was a matter of life and death.One's actions are based on a belief that something will happen and so one acts accordingly.

It is against this background that the actions of the missionaries should be considered. In the majority of cases, missionaries believed (and still do believe) that they had a special calling from God to 'spread the word' to indigenous people throughout the world. Of course, some may have had ulterior motives, as there are always 'bad apples' and situations are never black and white, but hence the large number of missionaries that were despatched to various countries. It is interesting to note that these missionaries came from a variety of backgrounds. One of these was C.T. Studd, who was educated at Eton, came from an extremely wealthy family and played cricket for England. He donated his inheritance to Christian organisations and became a missionary in China.

Christians have been accused of being aloof and arrogant regarding their beliefs. Why should Christianity be better than any other religion? Surely, all beliefs should be regarded as having an equal status? But if one truly believes the words of Christ, it is very difficult not to do one's best to ensure that his words are delivered to people throughout the world.

It is against this background of belief that various missionary organisations arrived in Kenya. I have described some of the dangers they faced, but some missionaries have gone to extraordinary lengths amongst indigenous people to achieve their goals. Female missionaries and nuns have suffered unbelievable indignities and have then continued with their work. Many missionaries have died excruciatingly painful deaths because they have believed that they are following the commands of their saviour. Unfortunately, this genuine belief and resultant ambition creates a dilemma. Should Christians be imposing their beliefs on anyone, let alone indigenous people, many of whom could be regarded as uneducated and therefore unable to refute what they are being told? As mentioned previously, missionaries arrive with 'goodies' that may appear to be part of the new religion that is being offered.

In the Western world, attitudes towards religion have changed in recent times. In the United Kingdom, it is not permissible for anyone to 'indoctrinate' another person into Christianity or any other religion. One has the freedom to express one's beliefs to whomsoever should wish to listen, but one cannot do more. During the nineteenth century, there were many preachers, like the Wesley brothers, who were extremely persuasive in their discourses. Had they been alive today, they would almost certainly have been prevented from expounding their beliefs and may well have been arrested if they had persisted!

It is also interesting to point out that despite becoming Christians and regular churchgoers, often those from the indigenous tribes in Kenya are still more likely, when a member of their family is sick, to visit the local witch doctor in preference to the local medical centre. Often Christian beliefs have to coexist with traditional ones, which makes one wonder about the sincerity of their new beliefs!

It is easy to criticise missionaries for what they have done, but they have also been the conduits of many excellent attributes and have suffered many hardships in the process. We also have to remember that it is not possible to 'undo' the past. We must learn from both the positives and the negatives.

Before ending the chapter, I include a short section on the life of Father Joya, who has been a key player in all that has happened.

Father Joya

Father Joya was born in a small village called Asinge, not far from the border with Uganda. His initial career path took him into sales and marketing. At one stage, he was involved in a project for the Kenyan Ministry of Agriculture that was investigating soil erosion. He also worked on a joint project for the Finnish and Kenyan governments, which involved establishing sites for boreholes in the area in which he was born. He did also take a job as a sales representative, but it was at this time that he felt the call to become a Consolata missionary so yet more studying was required. He was ordained as a priest in 1998, which was when he was posted to Loiyangalani, originally as an assistant parish priest and becoming priest-in-charge in 2000. He remained in Loiyangalani until 2003. He visited England in 2003, which was when I first met him. He had a variety of roles within the Consolata mission, culminating in the Regional Superior for the Consolata Missionaries in Kenya and Uganda, a role he served for two terms from 2011 until 2016. He was the first Kenyan to hold this position, which shows the high esteem with which the organisation regarded him. Since then, he has been studying for a doctorate, and in 2022 he was appointed Bishop of the Catholic Diocese of Maralal. Considering he once worked as a cashier at a local service station, his achievements have been extraordinary. He is a very private individual for whom his relationship with God is his foremost priority. It has been a privilege to have known and been associated with him over the years.

CHAPTER TWELVE

Intervention

In this chapter, I will discuss the concept of 'intervention'. I consider the way in which the colonial settlement intervened and changed the lives and destiny of the people of Kenya. I then address the issues of cultural intervention where the aim is to change the cultural habits of the people.

Colonial Settlement

Colonialism has received very negative press in recent years. I intend to show that there are, in fact, both positive and negative outcomes to be experienced by the intervention of those from outside Africa. Even with the advantage of hindsight, those seeking to change circumstances 'for the better' need to tread warily and consider carefully the results of any planned intervention.

Before the Europeans arrived in the nineteenth century and decided to carve up Africa amongst themselves, there were no 'countries' as we know them. Various tribes existed side by side in locations that had vague boundaries. These were sometimes observed and sometimes not. Severe drought that resulted in the loss of large numbers of livestock initiated intertribal raids, with the stronger tribes plundering the resources of the weaker tribes. There appears to have been little desire to overrun the areas of neighbouring tribes in an effort to extend the territory of any particular tribe. Over the years, tribes may well have been annihilated by neighbours, but it is more likely that weaker tribes were assimilated into stronger tribes as a result of intermarriage. Languages and customs of neighbouring tribes are often not dissimilar. Usually, tribes managed to survive raids from neighbouring stronger tribes and make good their losses, especially if they lived in areas that were less accessible to their neighbours.

There were tribes that had undesirable customs that proved especially hard on their neighbours. One tribe in northern Kenya required a particularly unpleasant ritual from its warriors as a rite of progress to manhood. They were required to emasculate an unfortunate individual from a neighbouring tribe, presenting proof of the deed to the elders. Naturally, young men from the tribe that was preyed upon lived in constant fear of becoming the next target for this rather shocking ritual. One actually wonders how the neighbouring tribe managed to survive if most of its males were unable to reproduce!

Although wealth and status related to the size of one's herd of animals, there was little desire to increase the size of these herds beyond manageable numbers, as the stock had to be fed and watered, so the desire to own vast quantities of livestock was rarely a consideration.

The fact that survival was not easy ensured that tribes appeared to be disinterested in acquiring vast areas of lands from weaker neighbours. The history of the majority of the African continent is very different from that of Europe. Our history consists of one major conflict after another. There was always at least one European leader keen to appeal to his or her subjects by seeking to acquire additional land from a neighbour. Throughout history, subjugating areas of a neighbouring country was the easiest means by which critics at home could be appeased! The overrunning of additional territory often resulted in the severe treatment of those unfortunate enough to reside in the area. Pillaging and raping seemed to be regarded as a legitimate consequence of conquest (still apparent in the war in Ukraine). The fact that humans, throughout most of history, have regarded other humans as being expendable is, to me, an extremely sad and distasteful aspect of our existence. In this respect, the more savage tribes in Africa were no different from their counterparts in other countries. In particular, both the Masai and the Turkana tribes were feared by their neighbours for their brutality.

After many thousands of years of relative stability, the majority of the African continent was to experience a dramatic change within the space of comparatively few years. Colonisation started at the end of the nineteenth century, and within less than a hundred years, not only had the countries changed beyond all recognition, but they had managed to shake off their colonial rulers and become independent.

Intervention in the Kenyan interior started with the construction of the railway from Uganda, the source of the Nile, to Mombasa on the coast. Mombasa had been an important staging post for trade of various sorts, but particularly the slave trade. In fact, one of the first actions the British took upon their annexation of this area of East Africa was to end this trade. The building of the railway was an incredible achievement in itself, although it was costly both financially and in terms of human suffering. Its apparent purpose was to facilitate transport across Kenya and provide protection for the source of the Nile, which was regarded as paramount for the fortunes of the British Empire. Initially, this project, together with the influx of settlers and the installation of a colonial government, had little effect on the Lake Turkana region. However, as the border with Ethiopia became the source of dispute, outposts were established in the north of the country that were manned by officials from the colonial office.

The introduction of law and order of sorts in the region was actually met with varied reactions from the local tribes. The weaker tribes who had been persecuted by their neighbours welcomed the new regime as they could now live without continual threats from their neighbours. On the other hand, the more dominant and savage tribes resented this curb on their freedom to persecute the weaker tribes. The government officials posted to the north of the country were for ever intervening in disputes and reprimanding tribes for encroaching on areas that belonged to their neighbours. Apparently, on one occasion a government officer was meeting with a group of Turkana, telling them forcibly that every tribe must remain in its own land; the Turkana spokesman said that it was an excellent idea and would "His Excellency please start with the white tribe?"! The presence of a relative semblance of law and order was appreciated as recently as the 1970s. Stephen Pern was the first to complete a total circumnavigation of Lake Turkana, accompanied by a few donkeys and local guides. The majority of the journey was accomplished with few setbacks. However, their passage through Ethiopia was fraught with difficulty. Despite having procured the correct permits, they were prevented from a safe passage by the Ethiopian officials stationed on the border. In fact, the lawlessness in Ethiopia was such that they felt threatened by the volatile nature of the situation, so much so that they were forced to take drastic measures to proceed with their journey. This involved a forced march in the middle of the night to cross at a secret location the river that had proved to be a barrier to legitimate progress. Once safely across the border back into Kenya, one of the guides remarked that he was glad that Kenya had been colonised by the British and that they had managed to instil a sense law and order in the country, unlike the Ethiopians.

This is not the book to be considering all the pros and cons of the colonisation. There is no doubt that aspects have been rightly criticised, but I think it is worth making a few points on both sides of the debate.

There is little doubt that the majority of those involved in the process of colonisation regarded themselves as a superior race, endeavouring to instil their values and beliefs on people who required education. Speaking about Kenya, which was obviously colonised by the British, many of those arriving in the country were the product of a class system in their country of origin. They were therefore establishing a system in Kenya that was based on this class system in the United Kingdom. The Kenyans were to be exploited in the same way in which those from the lower classes in the United Kingdom were exploited. Indigenous Kenyans were employed as labourers on the farms and as servants in the households of the settlers. In some cases they were treated poorly and in others very well. Being employed as servants ensured that many Kenyans had access to opportunities only dreamt about by their contemporaries who were unemployed. I mentioned earlier that my mother was raised in Kenya. I can cite two incidents that illustrate the loyalty between employer and employee.

During the Mau Mau unrest in the 1950s, when Kenyans and settlers suffered atrocious outrages, my grandparents had a beautiful house and gardens in one of the more affluent suburbs of Nairobi. The property was surrounded by security fencing with watchmen employed on a round-the-clock basis to guard the property. One of the watchmen employed by my grandparents was approached by members of the Mau Mau and given a choice. He was told that he must arrange for the gate to be left unlocked at a specific time so that entry could be gained in order to murder my grandparents and their servants. If he failed, this young man's family members would be brutally killed. The following day, the young man was discovered hanging from a tree. His loyalty to my grandparents was such that he could not do what he had been asked, so he had taken his own life.

My grandmother lived to be over ninety. At the time of her death, she had a devoted servant called Dickson. He had worked for my grandmother for a considerable number of years and was devoted to her. He told me that he was prepared to do anything for her. Through her generosity and kindness, not only had he managed to acquire his own house, but each of his children had been educated. He was so grateful for being given the opportunity to work for her, because many of his friends, who had not been employed in similar circumstances, could only dream about his fortunate position. He was devastated when she died, but being of fairly advanced years himself, she had ensured he was well looked after for the duration of his life. Kenya is not a welfare state. Kenyans must earn money to survive. As in the United Kingdom, there were, and still are, jobs which are arduous, unpleasant and underpaid, but in Kenya it is better to be earning money than to be out of work.

Having said this, exploitation was rife. From a very early stage, there were voices calling for a partnership with a view to promoting an independent country run and organised by the Kenyans. Unfortunately, there was a considerable degree of arrogance and many of these voices were ignored. The indigenous people were regarded as a cheap source of labour, which facilitated an easy flow of income. It is incredible to think that many of these people who had virtually nothing were taxed! To make matters worse, money raised from taxation in the early years was not used in Kenya but was sent to the United Kingdom to bolster its coffers.

Collecting taxes was not straightforward, especially in the north of the country. As many Kenyans did not possess cash, taxation was often gathered 'in kind', i.e. in goats, camels or sheep. As many Kenyans were nomadic, government officers who were tasked with collecting the taxes often had an impossible task. Just as tax evasion is rife in this country, so it was in Kenya. Herds and flocks were known to diminish in size when taxes were due to be paid. Complete herds and whole families could suddenly vanish when the arrival of a tax collector was imminent. Unfortunately, if the owners were taken by surprise, endeavouring to partition one's herds so that a sizeable portion could 'disappear' was not easy. Quite how straightforward it would have been to conceal herds of bad-tempered camels or bleating goats, one can only guess. Just as trying to persuade a domesticated dog or cat in this country not to make a noise when one seeks an element of surprise is nigh on impossible, endeavouring to persuade a herd of goats to remain silent must have been even more difficult. There was a great deal of camaraderie amongst the animals, so not only were they very reluctant to leave the company of their mates but they often made their feelings known vociferously! Not a positive attribute when the owner was doing his best to partition his herd or conceal them. Subterfuge had to be planned in advance, no doubt similar to what happens with tax evasion in this country!

What was actually achieved, whether by correct or incorrect means, over a hundred years was incredible. From a country that had no infrastructure (Nairobi did not exist until it became a railway siding at the beginning of the twentieth century) to the time of independence in the 1960s, it had changed beyond belief. It is interesting to ponder what might have happened had none of the European countries decided to 'carve up' Africa. How would the various tribes have managed to cooperate to build a country or countries? Obviously, boundaries between countries would have been more sensitive to the tribal boundaries. Unfortunately, when the colonials arrived and delineated boundaries, they thought little about the impact these boundaries would have on the individual tribes. Take, for example, the boundary between Kenya and Tanzania. It looks very much as if a civil servant in an office has taken out a ruler and drawn a straight line without a thought as to who might be affected by this line. This boundary commences at Lake Victoria, transcends the country diagonally until reaching and skirting Mount Kilimanjaro before proceeding directly to the coast. In doing so, it bisects the traditional Masai lands, some of which become part of Kenya and others part of Tanzania. As it happens, Mount Kilimanjaro was initially part of Kenya until Queen Victoria decided to give it to the Kaiser as a birthday present!

Without the presence of colonial powers, would Africa have become the United States of Africa with many little tribal countries? The idea that tribes should integrate, live peacefully and unite to form a single country is very much a European twentieth-century concept. Nevertheless, the African countries would cease to function if the individual tribes remained in their traditional areas without some form of cooperation. There is no doubt that Kenyans are now hugely proud of their country. Yes, there are tribal issues, which I will consider shortly, but one only has to experience the reaction of Kenyans when one of their athletes wins a gold medal at a sporting event to see the pride that they have in their country. This pride extends to their flag and their national anthem. They may be a young country, but they are a proud country.

Granted, tribal membership remains to be of supreme importance. This is particularly obvious in events such as elections. Politicians rely on votes from the members of their tribe. It is no accident that the country is run by a President from the dominant tribe, Kikuyu. A Samburu or

Turkana President would be most unlikely unless a politician emerged from one of these tribes who could gather support via an alliance with other tribes to curtail this domination. The smaller tribes do not have the political power to promote one of their number to attain the highest office in the country. Having one of one's own in power was of great benefit to other members of the tribe. Just as politicians in most countries reward their 'cronies', the situation is no different in countries like Kenya. It would not be surprising if many of the ideas concerning corruption had originally been learned from the colonials!

There is no doubt that corruption is rife in Kenya, as illustrated in the scenario in my most recent visit to the country. However, we are aware that it is not exactly unknown in this country either. There is no doubt that when pursuing a job, it is still not what you know but often who you know that is of greater importance. Vacancies are supposedly advertised to give applicants from outside a chance, but often someone internally has been earmarked for the position before the applications have been processed, let alone interviews conducted. In Kenya, suddenly being in a position of importance where one has authority over others opens the door to many financial opportunities. Accepting bribes or 'inducements' has become a way of life.

Before condemning such practices, it is necessary to consider carefully how often we may have been conducting our financial transactions in a manner that could be considered to have been underhand. Paying cash to avoid VAT is, in fact, defrauding the government. Perhaps this is something the reader may have done? I can see you reaching for your cheque books and magnanimously saying that you will give the money saved to charity. Before you do so, think carefully, because you might inadvertently compound the deception. Your charitable donation is probably subject to a gift aid claim, so not only have you defrauded the government out of its legitimate VAT, but you have also compelled it to pay out gift aid on the money that should have been theirs in the first place!

In order to sustain all that is needed to ensure that the country can survive and function requires considerable expertise and proficiency. Countries like the UK have developed over centuries, supposedly learning from mistakes and ensuring changes to better the lives of their citizens. Kenyans have had to learn everything in a comparatively short space of time. Much of what they have learnt has come from the colonial system that grew during the twentieth century. Take one aspect of this. When the British arrived, each tribe had its own language, none of which was in a written form. One of the languages, Swahili, was to become the common language. The standardisation of communication was non-existent. One has to return to the twelfth and possibly thirteenth centuries to recall the last time there was a similar problem in England.

The colonials did bring with them ideas, skills and a desire to update the facilities. Roads and a railway were constructed. Houses, schools and medical facilities were introduced to the country. It was, in fact, access to education that probably had the most profound effect on the indigenous Kenyans, enabling them to acquire the skills necessary to gain their independence. New crops, such as tea, coffee and pyrethrum, were introduced experimentally.

Exploitation of people is one thing, but certainly on a par is the exploitation of resources. Vast areas of the country were requisitioned to be allocated to settlers, initially mainly from South Africa. Although the farming was not always profitable in the early years, there is no doubt that over time the resources offered by this country have ensured healthy profits for individuals and companies with little return for the indigenous Kenyans. In addition, the exploitation of resources is lamentable, especially when these resources are wild animals.

The ivory trade had flourished long before the arrival of the British. Ironically, the decimation of the local wildlife was curtailed by the colonial government. Nevertheless, when Europeans first ventured into the interior of the country, it was teeming with wildlife. Rhinoceros and elephant were present in vast numbers. Lion were so plentiful that they regarded many of the unfortunate workers building the railway from Mombasa to Uganda as easy pickings for their daily meal. Humans tend to run more slowly than impala and therefore are easier to catch!

It was the ivory trade, though, that fuelled the greatest slaughter. Although, from early on, permits were required, the trade in ivory was so rewarding that illicit hunting flourished. To this day, poaching remains a significant problem, despite the ban on the trading of ivory. Those trading legally justified their actions by stating that they only killed the largest members of the species. Of course, once the giants had disappeared, the 'largest' members of any species became smaller and smaller. 'Trophy' hunting gained in popularity so that money could be earnt by organising private hunting expeditions. When visiting Loiyangalani, it is difficult to imagine that elephant, rhinoceros and lion, to mention a few species, roamed freely throughout the area. I am not sure what would happen if one of the magnificent elephants of yesteryear encountered one of the three hundred and sixty-five wind turbines that have replaced them!

It is interesting to note that Jacob was full of praise for the British colonials. After independence, maintenance of much of the infrastructure that had been established by the British – roads, railways, schools and hospitals – had lapsed under successive regimes. It is now the Chinese who are stepping into the breach to carry out the maintenance that is so desperately needed. The burning question is, at what price in the long term? Jacob pointed out that corruption was still more of a problem than it had been under colonial rule. He did more than hint that there are those in the country who believe that Kenya would be better off if it had remained under British control. He pointed out that of all the colonial powers that had had interests in the African continent, the British were the most preferable. He described some rather gruesome practices that other European powers used when dealing with the locals, some of which reminded me of conditions in the United Kingdom in the Middle Ages, when punishments were exceptionally horrendous. It was a most interesting insight given the anticolonial feeling that is so widespread in the United Kingdom at present.

Suffice it to say, what has happened has happened. There can be no turning back of the clock. Although the tribes in northern Kenya were left very much to their own devices in the early years, during the latter half of the twentieth century, things were to change dramatically, even for them.

For many tribal elders, there has always been a desire to maintain the status quo. They have lived in the same manner for many years. Their way of life, though not without hardships, has ensured their survival. In chapter 9, I alluded to current comparisons between those living beside Lake Turkana and those living in the United Kingdom. It is also interesting to consider the comparative lifestyles in the early nineteenth century of, say, a Turkana with that of someone endeavouring to survive in the slums of London. At that time, England may well have been considered to be 'civilised'. However, many people lived in appalling conditions with no sanitation, disease, and at times little or no food or heating. Given these circumstances, would not the better option be life as a nomad roaming the plains of Kenya with one's family and livestock? Admiring the sunset over Lake Turkana would have been infinitely preferable to trying to locate the sun over a smog-infested River Thames!

Going back another three or four hundred years, the conditions for the lower classes in England were far worse, with further dangers from marauding armies and the ever-present threat from outlaws and other criminals. At that time in Kenya, conditions for the Turkana tribesman would have been much the same as they were so many years later.

Progress comes in many guises. In the present day the ability of the local inhabitants to move around their country would seem to be advantageous. Food, especially fruit and vegetables, can be purchased from other parts of the country. Medicine can be acquired for the sick. Building materials can be delivered for better accommodation and schools. What if, however, in bringing these products to the community, those transporting the goods also bring diseases like Aids? This very real danger has been highlighted by the recent Coronavirus pandemic. Because Loiyangalani is sufficiently remote, there have been no recorded cases in the community. Travel to and from the area has been severely restricted, which has ensured the community has been kept safe. As restrictions are lifted, in all probability the virus will reach the community. They cannot remain isolated for ever.

Of course, living in a concrete dwelling is preferable to living in a thatched hut. Having access to a variety of food instead of solely maize and goats should ensure a healthier diet. Wearing decent clothes instead of being dressed in tattered hand-me-downs builds self-esteem. Having access to medical facilities saves lives. Even counting one's wealth in money instead of goats has its advantages. At least money does not die when there is a drought! Many people would advocate these changes, as overall they offer positive changes to the lives of these people.

In addition to this, there has been the advance of new ideas and beliefs which challenge their centuries-old customs. As mentioned in the previous chapter, the arrival of the Consolata mission and indeed other missionaries heralded not only the opportunity for education and improvements in their health but also a new faith, Christianity. The big question that arises concerns the degree to which those from outside should advocate change. Some change appears beneficial but may not actually be as positive as it first appears. Some change is controversial but generally considered to be necessary by those bringing the change. Other change is controversial but perceived to be necessary by certain members of the society. Anyone wishing to interfere needs to tread very carefully. As has been seen, some ideas that on the surface may have been perceived to be advantageous have actually failed to provide the desired outcomes, often through the lack of sustainability. There are, however, other hidden pitfalls to 'good' ideas.

What if the changes advocated interfere with the customs and culture of the tribes? I have discussed changes in beliefs as advocated by the introduction of Christianity. It is time to consider how to implement changes to customs that are generally regarded as unacceptable or even barbaric.

Cultural Intervention

Before considering these customs, it is necessary to explain the 'betrothal' and 'marriage' process.

Young girls are often promised to men who are considerably older than they are and who usually already have one or more wives. They can tempt the parents of the young girls to hand over their daughters as wives in exchange for a certain number of goats. If the family is poor, the parents will succumb to the opportunity to increase their wealth.

Alternatively, a luckier young girl will be betrothed to a young man of approximately the same age in a 'beading' ceremony. Beaded items are handed over as a sign of betrothal in the same way that an engagement ring will be purchased in this country. Once betrothed, the pair will expect to be married eventually, but even having been 'beaded', young girls can find themselves exploited by older men if the price is right!

Jacob has added:

> The cultural practice of 'beading' of girls by young men, called 'warriors', is done to facilitate early marriages and also promotes polygamy. This early courtship is an agreement between the parents of a young man and the girl which allows them to have a boyfriend/girlfriend relationship. In this arrangement, the young man brings some beads to the girl in her parents' home to mark the beginning of the relationship. Young warriors usually bring several packets of beads which are made into necklaces that are worn by the girl. Although the young girl and warrior live separately in their parents' homes, the arrangement allows them to engage in intimate relations, which may lead to pregnancy and even early marriages. Since there is no guarantee that the beaded girl will be married to the warrior who beaded her, she may be rejected and then married to an old man if she becomes pregnant.

Marriage is an important event in the lives of the young people, but before this happens, they are required to undergo a process that has been widely criticised but has been regarded by some tribes as a cultural necessity. The El Molo, Samburu and Rendille tribes in the area have traditionally circumcised males and females. The Turkana do not indulge in this practice. It is this circumcision process, particularly regarding females, that has caused so much controversy.

The circumcision of males is also practised by the Jewish community throughout the world. It is therefore not the practice itself that is regarded as unacceptable but the way in which it is carried out. Jewish children are circumcised at a very young age, with the operation being conducted in a sterilised environment within a hospital. Circumcision ceremonies in Kenya usually involve the circumcision of more than one male at any one time. These young men are of adolescent age. No anaesthetics are used. The operation is usually performed by a tribal elder using the same unsterilised cutting implement for each young man. Each individual experiences considerable pain and the wound may often become infected. The tribes advocating this custom believe that it is part of an initiation ceremony mandatory for all males entering adulthood. As caring adults, outsiders can point out the negative aspects of this operation, but the question remains: do we have the right to interfere with the customs of the particular tribe? If they remain adamant that the custom is to continue, the logistics of ensuring that each operation is carried out safely and securely in a hospital environment are considerable. There are no hospitals within easy reach, and such operations would be beyond the financial resources of these people. It is hard to explain that male circumcision is permissible for certain members of society because they have the means to ensure the procedure is carried out safely and hygienically, whereas for those whose techniques are dangerous and unhygienic it should not be permitted. It is exceedingly difficult to change a custom that is regarded as highly significant, even though it is perceived to be dangerous and consequently unacceptable.

The situation is far worse when considering female circumcision, which can rightly be regarded as barbaric. The process is known as Female Genital Mutilation (FMG). This is not the place to offer graphic descriptions of the process, except to state that there are three degrees of FMG that are practised by various tribes in Kenya, all of which involve the 'cutting' of parts of the female genitalia and then 'stitching' to decrease the size of the orifice. It is believed that the practice evolved to ensure the chastity of the females and does not have quite the cultural significance of male circumcision. The operation is generally performed on young girls using equipment that is unsterilised, without the use of any form of anaesthetic. The girls suffer significant loss of blood. The wound can become infected, and the mortality rate of the girls recovering from the procedure or endeavouring to give birth having had the procedure is disconcertingly high. Depending upon which of the three 'operations' has been used, the young women may well continue to experience problems throughout their lives, especially when giving birth. There is no doubt that the procedure is nothing short of barbaric, and the practice has been outlawed not only by the Kenyan government but also by governments in other countries where the procedure is practised.

It would seem that the practice is so outrageous that persuading tribes to cease performing the operation should be relatively straightforward, but there is an interesting problem. In many cultures, it is the men who make the decisions as to what should and should not take place regarding their women. FGM is an exception. It is the women who insist on their daughters undergoing this process. They believe that it is in their interest to perpetuate the custom. It may seem bizarre that women who have themselves often suffered horrendous problems in childbirth should insist that their daughters undergo the same procedures, which may lead to complications which they too have experienced when giving birth. Why is this so? Daughters are, unfortunately, expendable. They are used, as has been mentioned previously, as a potential source of income via the dowry that is handed over by a prospective husband. These girls need to be virgins in order to attract significant dowries from their suitor. Girls who have engaged in premarital sex are perceived to be 'defective goods'. FGM is performed so that young girls are less likely to engage in premarital sexual activity. FGM is regarded as a form of contraception. Because the girls are less likely to have sexual relationships, they are less likely to become pregnant before marriage. Once the dowry has been paid, the young girl is no longer of any value to her family. If she is to die in childbirth, this would be regarded at most to be unfortunate, but would in no way affect the financial position of her family. Also, there are other young women from which the young man can select another wife. It is a very sad state of affairs, but in many families, wealth in goats is of greater importance than any emotional ties between parents and their children. This may in part relate to the rate of infant and childhood mortality, which in years past has been high. Perhaps, in some cases, parents have been reluctant to create very strong bonds with their offspring because they believe their children may not survive.

Fortunately, with mortality rates decreasing, the situation is changing slowly, but young girls are often still regarded only in light of their commercial potential. It is exceedingly difficult to change perceptions, especially when the families cannot visualise the alternatives. In addition, it is necessary to highlight the fact that in many cultures which one would perceive to be well-educated, women continue to be perceived as inferior to their male counterparts. Arranged marriages, where families attempt to whisk their daughters away to other countries in order to marry someone who has been selected on their behalf because the arrangement has been deemed to be beneficial to her family, remain a distinct possibility for young girls from certain cultural backgrounds. If cultural practices cannot be changed amongst those who have been educated, the chances of changing them in communities that are less well educated remain low. FMG is a significant part of the problem, but a change to the mindset of these communities continues to be a hurdle of considerable size. Jacob, in a previous section, has highlighted the problem when indicating that parents cannot visualise the long-term benefits of change. If today a father is offered a specific number of goats in exchange for his daughter's hand in marriage, he cannot understand that rejecting the offer and allowing his daughter to continue with her education could bring more goats in the future. In five years, she could be earning a salary that increases significantly the number of goats owned by the family. The situation is such that the immediacy of financial gain is still seen to be paramount. A family needs feeding today. What may happen in the future is extremely difficult for them to contemplate. I initially experienced the same doubts when asking the women to part with their wares without payment so that I could sell them overseas. Investment in the future is not an easy concept for these people. Even educated people in this country often struggle to understand the benefits of investment in the future.

The desire is to increase the status and position of the women in Kenya. The first task is to eradicate the highly undesirable practice of FMG. In doing this, it must be stressed that the aim is to terminate a procedure that brings inconceivable pain and trauma to young girls, something that is simply unacceptable in the world as we know it. Unlike male circumcision, the process does not have its roots in strong cultural beliefs or rituals.

It can be argued that the changing of cultural practices which are perceived as harmful may need to be modified to ensure that they become safe or abandoned totally. What should be the procedure regarding cultural beliefs? This is, by nature, extremely controversial and one has to tread very carefully for fear of upsetting people. There are those who argue that cultural beliefs should remain as they are without external interference, but if these beliefs bring harm or pain to youngsters, surely they cannot be permitted to continue.

Summary

By and large, the people of Kenya were relatively content with their way of life until the changes at the end of the last century. It is the younger members of the tribes that are advocating change. They have access to the outside world via mobile phones and the internet. They can see what is happening not only in other parts of their country but also in other countries of the world, and they wish to be part of the action. They have aspirations and desires. They have also experienced the presence of visitors from other lands who have possessions about which they can only dream.

Even if it is generally agreed that these changes are for the best, a transition is required. Such a transition is fraught with problems, some of which were mentioned by Jacob. Selling every goat overnight is not an option, so goats have to be cared for. Certain members of the family are obliged to fill this role. Decisions have to be made as to who should be educated and who should miss out. Even if every child attends primary school, which is now free, many families do not possess the resources to fund one child, let alone several children to attend secondary school or further education. Unemployment is already high in the country. The prospects for many of the children, even if fully educated, still remain low. If education does not bring prosperity to all, then how can families be convinced that the necessary sacrifices will actually help their children? Surely, it is better to keep the goats and allow the boys to tend the herds, and use the girls to bring wealth to the family by marrying rich suitors. The word 'sustainable' emerges yet again. If the push for education does not bring the desired prosperity to all families, it is very difficult to persuade them to abandon their customary practices and embrace new ideas. The changes advocated would generally be considered as desirable, with the long-term aim to change old practices so that the children can look forward to a more prosperous future.

Intervention is a very complex issue. Even changes that initially seem to be of benefit may in fact be the source of hidden dangers. One has to consider carefully the effects of any changes that may be introduced. All people have basic human rights and these need to be considered before taking the decision to intervene with any new idea or project.

CHAPTER THIRTEEN

Support and Sustainability

In this final chapter, I wish to consider what one might aim to achieve when contemplating supporting an individual, a family or indeed a community in a country where there is a desperate need for assistance.

The safest way to sponsor a child is through one of the larger charities. Although it is not always easy to establish exactly how much of one's donation actually reaches the individual child, there is no doubt that the power of collective giving can change whole communities in a dramatic way.

If one travels, as I did, to a specific region in a specific country, it is easy to be overwhelmed by the deprivation in that location. One can only afford to support one or possibly two families. How does one select which family to support? Is there any point in giving very limited assistance? Surely, it is better to walk away and do something else with one's money. In my view, decisions were made more difficult by the fact that Loiyangalani is so inaccessible that it is beyond the reach of the larger charities "(although recently there have been signs that the situation is changing). These charities must justify their expenses. It is therefore easier for them to work within sensible travelling distance of the major cities, so that supplies and equipment can be obtained and conveyed without the addition of considerable transportation costs.

So, what happened to me? Why have I persevered in the manner in which I have? What have I been seeking to achieve through the formation of my charity? As mentioned previously, initially the charity was established solely to ensure that I could reclaim gift aid on my donations to assist one individual with his education. Since then, the charity has snowballed and achieved more than I had ever imagined could have been possible.

It should be clear through the discussions in the previous chapters that one has to be very careful with what one seeks to change. Improving the life of one individual who will have a family of his/her own, producing children who will then have families themselves, all of whom will have benefitted directly from the original sponsorship of the first individual, is always a positive outcome. It is an investment in the future of a family that will continue to manifest itself and grow long after one has passed away. Selecting a possible beneficiary, one needs to tread very carefully, utilising the advice of local people who can explain to others the rationale behind the decision. This was the procedure I adopted when selecting Albert upon my return to Loiyangalani after helping members of David's family.

If the situation is then subject to change in that the formation of an official charity offers the opportunity for further sponsorship from interested parties, the selection process requires more thorough scrutiny. Once my committee and I had decided to focus on supporting students from the Loiyangalani Primary School, we needed the beneficiaries to have been selected on the basis of a set of criteria agreed upon by ourselves and a committee in Loiyangalani itself. Bosco, who was headmaster at the time, required the support of other members of the community in order to be able to justify the choice of beneficiaries.

It was important not to introduce any criteria or restrictions based on our beliefs. For example, being a Christian was not a prerequisite. Although we disapproved of practices like FGM, we did not wish to exclude members of families from tribes who practised this procedure. Although we were happy to express our opinions when asked, it was not our place to physically change the situation within any particular family. We were aware that offering children the opportunity for education did impose hardships on various families. The goats needed tending. They were still keen to reap the financial benefits of dowries from their daughters. Our aim was to demonstrate that we wished to offer an alternative to the customary way of life, but whether or not this was to be accepted by individual families was to be a family or community decision. The desire for change should come from the community and not be imposed by outsiders who just happen to have the resources to implement change that may or may not be what the community desires. Being a facilitator for change requires guidance from the local people. Help must be channelled in an appropriate manner so that the local community is involved in the decision-making process. Each term, the committee in Loiyangalani meets with the headmaster and creates a 'wish list' of items that they regard to be of importance at that particular time. These items are presented in what the committee perceives to be the order of importance. We decide how much we can afford to donate at any given moment, thereby funding items in the order in which they are presented. Inevitably, one or two of the least important items on the list may not be funded at that time and must wait until resources have been obtained.

The members of the committee in Loiyangalani select the students from the primary school who are to be put forward for sponsorship. They consider those who have performed well, who are likely to work hard, and who come from families who would not otherwise be able to fund their education. At the same time, they endeavour to ensure that there is diversity regarding the tribe to which they belong. This balance is perhaps the most difficult aspect of the selection. It is not easy maintaining this balance, especially if students from one particular tribe are more likely to fulfil the criteria than those from another. At times decisions have been questioned by the locals and certain families have felt aggrieved by the selection process.

One also has to realise that despite rigorous selection processes, students do not perform as predicted and will, at times, not achieve the predicted grades. At times, there are circumstances beyond our control. Bereavement in a family may require a selected male student to return to his family to care for the livestock. Incapacitation of the mother in the family through an unexpected illness may require the eldest daughter in the family to forego her studies to care for younger siblings. One of the students being sponsored became pregnant. Once she had had her child, she asked if her sponsor could not only continue to fund her education but also provide money for childcare. This presented a considerable problem. If we say no, this appears harsh, as we do not know the circumstances under which she became pregnant. If we say yes, it may convey the idea that we condone the pregnancy, in which case other girls may regard pregnancy during their education as being acceptable and easily accommodated. As it happens, we managed to convey our concern regarding the situation, expressing our acceptance of what had happened but at the same time professing a strong desire to ensure that other females do all they can to avoid a repeat of the circumstances. Luckily, the young girl's sponsor was happy to continue to offer sufficient support to ensure that she acquired a skill rather than continue at school. She then used this skill to establish a small business and support her child. Fortunately, the scenario has not as yet been repeated.

My greatest concern regarding any of the projects that I undertake in relation to Loiyangalani is sustainability. I have already alluded to this earlier. I was not happy when I realised that the selling of the beaded items would have to end. At first it had been a relatively small endeavour, but it had soon escalated out of control into something bigger than I had originally anticipated and could not be sustained. Thankfully, the women had profited in ways far beyond their initial expectations. They had been able to build a compound from which there were multiple benefits.

Sustainability relates to both short-term aims and the long-term objectives. For instance, sponsoring a student is a short-term aim. Secondary education is generally a fixed cost and affordable for those who wish to become sponsors. A significant problem manifests itself when the student finishes secondary school and wishes to progress further. Those with good grades may wish to proceed to university, which for sponsors requires a financial commitment considerably larger than the initial pledge to cover the secondary school costs. For many, this is an undertaking they either cannot afford or do not wish to undertake. Many would rather sponsor another student. This creates a dilemma. Is the student to be abandoned at this stage? It may be possible to finance a short course so that the student can develop a skill, but for many this would fail to maximise their potential. Is it fair to raise the expectations of these students by offering finance at one level but not the next? The problem is compounded by the fact that some of us will support our students to university. This means that progress becomes a lottery depending upon whom has been selected as the sponsor. The issue of higher education has become a matter of great concern. If we cannot sustain support for a student until the ultimate goal is attained, should we even commence any form of financial assistance beyond primary school? The committee in England is, even now, implementing procedures that will provide manageable solutions to this problem.

There is also the long-term issue regarding sustainability. At present, those on the committee for the Loiyangalani Trust in England are of an age where we can reasonably expect the charity to continue to grow and assist the local community for a few more years at least. We are also aware that we need to enthuse younger people to join our organisation. It would be very hard on those in Loiyangalani if we had to commence winding up the operations because we had no one to continue our work.

Similarly, we have to be aware that we have had two very special headmasters in Loiyangalani, Bosco and Jacob, both of whom have worked hard to ensure that the aims and objectives are achieved, and that the money is channelled in the correct direction. What if Jacob moved from Loiyangalani Primary School? Would his successor not only be as trustworthy but also as willing to help as he has been? It is a time-consuming task and at times can be very challenging. The students can cause problems. Pressure is applied by those outside the scheme to be included. The long-term future of the charity depends on the committee in England and also on that in Loiyangalani.

We have been lucky. Because we are a small charity, accountability is relatively straightforward. Sponsors appreciate the fact that they can see their donations being used efficiently. Money is paid into the charity account. It is transferred to Kenya. The sponsored child attends school. Reports are sent back to England so that the sponsor observes the progress of the sponsored child. With larger charities, it is sometimes difficult to understand exactly how the money from one's donation is allocated and spent. Often, there are urgent appeals through the media for emergency relief. As mentioned previously, watching the horrific scenes on the television, one can rightly become appalled. The temptation is to reach for one's chequebook or one's phone to give a donation as a means of assisting. It is all too easy to believe that one has 'done one's bit', so that one's mind can then revert to more trivial matters such as whether one has remembered to put out the rubbish for collection or whether the potatoes are cooked. The advantage of a long-term commitment to a small charity is the realisation that one is playing an active role in what is happening. Loiyangalani is a relatively small community being supported by a relatively small number of people.

I wish to conclude by stating that I intend to remain involved, helping the school and sponsoring students, for as long as possible. It is when one visits Loiyangalani and observes the smiles of the children, feels the warmth of the community (and the sun!) and experiences the gratitude of all those who have benefitted from the scheme in some way that one realises why one does what one does.

Postscript

By now it is most certainly obvious to my readers that I am a committed Christian. I would like to point out to all my readers that there are two ways of considering the scenario that has taken place.

On many occasions I have been at the right place at the right time and have often met the right people at the right time. The Loiyangalani story would not have unfolded in the way that it did if any one of these events had not taken place.

Either this story is one of a happy series of coincidences or the hand of God has been playing an important role. It is for you to decide – but I know what I believe!

Bibliography

Brown, Monty; *Where Giants Trod;* Quiller Press, London (1989).

Chenevix Trench, Charles; *Men Who Ruled Kenya, the Kenya Administration 1892-1963;* Radcliffe Press, London (1993).

Hillaby, John; *Journey to the Jade Sea;* Paladin, St Albans (1973).

Kenyatta, Jomo; *Facing Mount Kenya;* Secker and Warburg, London (1959).

Ochieng, W.R.; *A Modern History of Kenya 1895-1980;* Evans Brothers, Nairobi (1989).

Pavitt, Nigel; *Kenya, A Country in the Making 1880-1940;* W.W. Norton & Co, New York (2008).

Pern, Stephen; *Another Land, Another Sea;* Victor Gollancz Ltd, London (1979).

Ruark, Robert; *Something of Value;* Hamish Hamilton, London (1955).

Ruark, Robert; *Uhuru;* Hamish Hamilton, London (1962).

Trevisiol, Alberto; *They Went Out to Plough the Field: Pages of History of The Consolata Missionaries in Kenya: 1902-1981;* unpublished at the time of writing

Also by Anthony Mitchell

Free Will
God's Choice, Our Choice

Onwards and Upwards Publishers
ISBN 978-1-78815-659-2

Free Will: God's Choice, Our Choice considers the implications of God's decision to grant freedom of choice to all humankind, and seeks to address questions such as: What exactly is free will? Why did God grant humankind free will? If humankind has free will, who is in charge, God or humans?

Using both real life experiences and hypothetical scenarios, A. E. Mitchell offers helpful explanations backed up with Scripture, for those who have puzzled over the relationship between God and evil. These are helpful suggestions as to how Christians can understand God's responses to prayer, interpret the Bible, deal with concepts such as fairness, forgiveness and judgement, and address issues such as sex and war.

Buy from the publisher by scanning the QR code below:

Or get your copy from any good bookshop.